EFT FOR THE
HIGHLY SENSITIVE
TEMPERAMENT

by Rue Anne Hass, MA

www.IntuitiveMentoring.com

Energy Psychology Press
P.O. Box 442
Fulton, CA 95439
www.energypsychologypress.com

Cataloging-in-Publication Data

Hass, Rue Anne.
EFT for the highly sensitive temperament / by Rue Anne Hass. —
1st ed.
    p. cm.
Includes index.
ISBN 978-1-60415-046-9
1. Anxiety sensitivity. 2. Emotional Freedom Techniques.
3. Temperment. 4. Sensitivity (Personality trait). I. Title.
RC531.H294 2009
616.85'223—dc22

20099030119

Cover design by Victoria Valentine
Editing by Stephanie Marohn
Typesetting by Karin Kinsey
Typeset in Cochin and Adobe Garamond
Printed in USA by Bang Printing
First Edition

10 9 8 7 6 5 4 3 2

Dedicated to all the highly sensitive people everywhere who are learning to deeply and completely love and accept themselves. The world needs what we know.

Contents

A Note to the Reader

A client I gave this book to in prepublication form wrote me an e-mail saying she couldn't read it—some of the stories were too restimulating of her own traumas. She said, "I hope in the future I will be able read the book and not get upset. Guess I'm just too sensitive!"

I suggested that she use Emotional Freedom Techniques (EFT), informally called "tapping," while she was reading it, tapping repeatedly up and down all the points in the EFT tapping sequence (see chapter 2). That turned out to be a good idea. She ended up reading the whole book, finding it very useful, and offering a list of grammar and spelling corrections! (Thank you!)

I recommend that you pay attention to your inner responses as you read, and take note of what specifically brings up an emotional reaction in you. Do the incredibly easy routine of EFT tapping while you read. Actually stop right then and tap for anything that makes you feel sad or fearful, or if you find yourself caught in a memory that restimulates feelings that you have been trying to keep buried.

If you take care of yourself while you explore this book, just the simple act of reading it can be a healing experience for you.

Introduction: Caring for the SPIRITED Self

There are lots of suggestions in this book for how to use Emotional Freedom Techniques (EFT). If you are new to tapping, as it is familiarly known, you might find this confusing. Take heart! Just let all the ideas and suggestions flow in to you as you read the book. Don't try to "learn" them all. Trust that they will all just naturally be at your fingertips as you develop your own style of doing EFT. This technique is not about "doing it right." It is about allowing the inner wisdom that is available to all of us, always, all ways, to flow toward the highest good.

I introduce you here to the central themes in this book about the highly sensitive temperament (HST), and how to use EFT to thrive when the world overwhelms you.

To heal what hurts, care for your SPIRITED self by tapping your truth. SPIRITED is an acronym for the characteristics of HST: *s*ensitivity, *p*ainful experiences from the past, *i*dentity limited by the resulting beliefs, *r*esponse to the limited identity, *i*ntention of the symptoms and emotions, the *t*ruth about you, the *e*vidence of your truth is all around, and *∂*irection.

Sensitivity

You are highly sensitive. Do you get overwhelmed, feel invisible or like an alien, or find ways to use your sensitivity to protect yourself? Does it seem like there is no one else like you out there, that no one understands? How do you feel about being "so sensitive"? Learn how to use EFT to change your experience.

*P*ainful Experiences from the Past

What broke your heart? Maybe it wasn't possible or safe to express what you felt.

Learn how to use EFT to heal your response to what happened.

*I*dentity Limited by the Resulting Beliefs

You came to believe that:

- There is something wrong with you.
- You are not enough.
- You feel things too deeply.
- It was your fault.
- Your needs aren't important.
- You have to save the world before you can be safe.
- You have to heal the world so that they (whoever "they" might be) can be safe.

- You have to justify being alive.

- You have been punished for being who you are or what you did.

- If you get what you want, you might not know who you are.

These beliefs have limited your identity, creating a cage in which you live. You have lost the feeling of being connected, of feeling like you belong. Learn how to use EFT to reframe your beliefs to positive thoughts that nourish and strengthen you, free your caged spirit, and give you a sense of belonging.

Response to the Limited Identity

Where does it hurt? Your body is holding all that pain and feeling. These are dark angels, messengers alerting you to the consequences of caging your identity. Stuffing what you felt and couldn't say can lead to chronic illness or self-sabotaging behaviors such as avoidance, procrastination, and addictions, Learn how to use EFT to heal the pain and give yourself other, better choices.

Intentions of the Symptoms and Emotions

Ask yourself: If I healed, what would I lose? If the hurt had a voice, what would it be saying? What is this feeling or symptom trying to get for you? Suggest to yourself: I can stand up for myself, express my own truth, ask for what I want. I deserve to take care of myself without feeling guilty! It is safe for me to be visible and be heard. Learn how to use EFT to install these deeper positive intentions.

The *T*ruth about You

- You were born good.
- You belong here.
- You are called to be here.
- You have a purpose here.
- You deserve to prosper.
- You are worthy of growing both spiritually and materially.
- It is OK to love and accept yourself.

Learn how to tap into your truth with EFT.

The *E*vidence of Your Truth Is All Around

Surprise, your goodness has always been there! Feed your soul. This is how you are good as gold. Be your natural state of wealth-being. Learn how to use EFT to uncover the evidence that you have been good all along.

*D*irection

Learn how to find the real yes and no in yourself. Use your body's responses as a compass. Point yourself in a healing, expanding direction. Learn how to use EFT to dissolve any inner fears about or objections to moving forward.

Be self-ish! Caring for your own spirit is your personal contribution to healing the soul of the Earth. Use EFT to generate the inner experience of deeply and completely loving and accepting yourself. This is your human birthright.

As you will see in the chapters that follow, people with highly sensitive temperaments take everything in more deeply than most people do. They feel emotions more deeply and feel pain more intensely. They worry more. They are more inclined to become overwhelmed and to blame themselves for what is going wrong in their lives. If you (or someone you know) have a highly sensitive temperament, EFT is a special blessing to you. It can help you not only ease and heal your physical and emotional pain, but also see and accept yourself differently. The world needs what you have to offer. You can use EFT to deepen, enhance, protect, honor, and make use of your sensitivity to improve your life and the life of the world.

1

How Do You Know If You Are a Highly Sensitive Temperament?

Have you ever heard (or said about someone else):

"Oh, you are just too sensitive!"

"You take things so hard!"

"Just let it roll off your back."

"Why can't you just let it go?"

"What's wrong with you? You are such a crybaby!"

You have probably thought they were right, that there must be something wrong with you. On the contrary, a highly sensitive temperament (HST) is a gift, and something you were likely born with. As psychologist Kyra Mesich, author of *The Sensitive Person's Survival Guide*, states, "Sensitive people are born that way. They were sensitive children." I believe sensitivity is a kind of awareness that can save the world. I speak as a "highly sensitive person" myself. It has taken me most of my life to understand this temperament and value it for its gifts. In my work as an intuitive mentor, I have worked with many people who are extra sensitive to stress, traumatic experiences, and environmental toxins. People with this temperament are also extraordinarily sensitive to beauty and spirituality, and they all have a desire to be a good custodian of the earth.

Attributes of the
Highly Sensitive Temperament (HST)

Does some (or all) of this describe you, or anyone you know?

- You feel emotions deeply, and you can't hide what you feel.

- You are always aware of what people around you are feeling.

- Your feelings are easily hurt by criticism or even a look, and you keep thinking about what happened, what you might have done wrong, and what you should have done instead.

- You feel deeply for other people's suffering. It is difficult for you to watch the news or a sad movie.

- You slip easily into feeling anxious or de-pressed, and once caught in the feeling, it is hard for you to move out of it.

- You are not comfortable in large crowds, hectic environments, or around loud music. You get easily overwhelmed when there is a lot going on.

- You want to be helpful, so much so that you put other people's needs ahead of your own.

- You do your best to avoid conflicts.

- You feel like an alien in your own family. Your family members are practical, industrious, and social, whereas you are quiet, imaginative, thoughtful, and creative.
- You are a perfectionist.
- You have a mission to bring peace to the world. You want to save the world from it-self. You can see how good things could be, if only ...
- You feel that your sensitivity is a weakness. You wish you were tougher and more thick-skinned.
- You wish things didn't bother you so much.
- You wish your emotions weren't so obvious to other people.
- You wish you could let things go and not worry so much.
- You often feel that you must hide your sensitivity from others.

The following are some of the many e-mail responses I received from people who read an article I wrote about the sensitive trait:

"When I first saw the words "sensitive person" I immediately thought, oh that's not me. but then I read on anyway, and by the end I was in tears. I think I am sensitive, and I used to get emotionally more upset about things so I learned to be hard and try to "not let things bother me." So now I have a host of some seriously debilitating health problems. Now I am "tough" emotionally and sensitive physically."

"Thank you for bringing this subject into our world and to the surface. I am a mom of three boys who I believe are sensitive, which…is not accepted in society too warmly. I want them to be able to share their gift with others."

"Oh Lord, this is where I need the help. I have all of the characteristics of emotional sensitivity—to the extreme."

"I hate being so overly sensitive and I take everything to heart…and it remains there for a very, very, very long time."

"I know you've heard this before but I swear you're writing about me. It's scary, but it helps too to realize that I'm not immature or selfish. I just feel more than most people and am hurt more easily than most. It's a very tough road, but I can't say that I'd trade for a personality that feels less."

"I no longer view myself as a high-maintenance freak. You've helped me by identifying me as highly sensitive. I feel it's very OK to be as cautious and self-protective as I am and, especially, that it's not something that I have to try and get over. I don't have to try and cure this before moving on in life because there's nothing to cure. I understand myself so much better now and that's such a good, comfortable feeling."

HST and Painful Experiences

Powerful memories often lie frozen in the past. The emotions associated with these memories can be triggered by present experiences, even small ones. Because sensitive people feel so much more deeply, these past experiences seem to define their identity, who they are in the world.

The following are basic concepts that underlie the healing and re-empowering that HSTs can experience with EFT:

- Painful experiences are felt more deeply by a sensitive person, especially as a child.

- Painful experiences lead to beliefs about who we are and what is possible for us in life.

- It may not be possible or safe to express the powerful anger, sadness, fear, and shame that we feel during and after these painful experiences.

- Those feelings get "stuffed" or swallowed.

- The stuffed feelings show up later in our lives as physical and emotional pain and illness.

- The people in our families who mistreated us did so because that is how they were treated, and these were the beliefs and feelings they themselves took on.

- The tendency to replicate these beliefs, feelings, and illnesses gets passed down through the generations of a family.

- The fear of confronting the powerful feelings stops us from beginning a healing journey.

- Our personal healing can begin to heal the whole family history.

HST Self-Test

To help you determine whether you are highly sensitive, take the self-test devised by Elaine Aron, therapist and author of many books and articles on the highly sensitive temperament. Though she doesn't incorporate EFT in her work, her insights regarding HST are very helpful.

Self-Test for the Highly Sensitive Person

Instructions: Answer each question according to the way you personally feel. Check the statement if it is at least somewhat true for you; leave unchecked if it is not very true or not at all true for you. You may have some or all of these characteristics.

__ I am easily overwhelmed by strong sensory input.

__ I seem to be aware of subtleties in my environment.

__ Other people's moods affect me.

__ I tend to be very sensitive to pain.

__ I find myself needing to withdraw during busy days, into bed or into a darkened room or any place where I can have some privacy and relief from stimulation.

__ I am particularly sensitive to the effects of caffeine.

__ I am easily overwhelmed by things like bright lights, strong smells, coarse fabrics, or sirens close by.

__ I have a rich, complex inner life.

__ I am made uncomfortable by loud noises.

__ I am deeply moved by the arts or music.

__ My nervous system sometimes feels so frazzled that I just have to go off by myself.

__ I am conscientious.

__ I startle easily.

__ I get rattled when I have a lot to do in a short amount of time.

__ When people are uncomfortable in a physical environment, I tend to know what needs to be done to make it more comfortable (like changing the lighting or the seating).

__ I am annoyed when people try to get me to do too many things at once.

__ I try hard to avoid making mistakes or forgetting things.

__ I make a point to avoid violent movies and TV shows.

__ I become unpleasantly aroused when a lot is going on around me.

__ Being very hungry creates a strong reaction in me, disrupting my concentration or mood.

__ Changes in my life shake me up.

__ I notice and enjoy delicate or fine scents, tastes, sounds, and works of art.

__ I find it unpleasant to have a lot going on at once.

__ I make it a high priority to arrange my life to avoid upsetting or overwhelming situations.

__ I am bothered by intense stimuli, like loud noises or chaotic scenes.

__ When I must compete or be observed while performing a task, I become so nervous or shaky that I do much worse than I would otherwise.

__ When I was a child, my parents or teachers seemed to see me as sensitive or shy.

Scoring: If you checked more than fourteen of the questions as true, you are probably highly sensitive. If fewer questions are true of you, but extremely true, that might also justify calling you highly sensitive.

Myers-Briggs INFP Personality Type

Another way to measure for sensitivity is through the Myers-Briggs Type Indicator (MBTI), which is based on the trait theory of personality and Carl Jung's earlier theory of psychological types. This assessment employs a questionnaire designed to measure psychological preferences in how people perceive the world and make decisions (see personalitypage.com). I think it is helpful to learn about a topic from many different angles, so I offer you this additional window into evaluating and considering what it means to be highly sensitive.

Though INFP (introverted, intuitive, feeling, perceiving) is the Myers-Briggs type associated with HST, there are infinite ways that personality characteristics can combine, stand out, or be masked. Though remarkably accurate, the MBTI is still a subjective measurement. I had a client who took the whole assessment and then burst into tears when she didn't show up in the scoring as a sensitive INFP. It turned out that when she took the test, she had answered the questions according to the way she thought she should feel rather than how she actually felt. It is typical of HSTs to try to follow the rules perfectly, even if the rules don't fit them!

The MBTI is based on the premise that we all have a primary mode of operation within four categories: 1) Our flow of energy is either Extraverted or Introverted; 2) How we take in information is either Sensing or Intuitive, 3) How we prefer to make decisions is via either Thinking or Feeling; and 4) Our preferred basic daily lifestyle is Judging or Perceiving.

According to Myers-Briggs assessment, the primary mode of living for INFPs is internally focused, that is, they deal with things according to how they feel about them, or how they fit into their personal value system. They also take things in primarily via their intuition.

INFPs are idealists and perfectionists who drive themselves hard in their quest of achieving the goals they have identified for themselves. They are thoughtful, considerate, and highly intuitive about people. They are on a continuous mission to find the truth and meaning underlying things. Every encounter and every piece of knowledge gained gets sifted through their value system, and is evaluated to see if it has any potential to help them define or refine their path in life. The goal at the end of the path is always the same: The INFP is driven to help people and make the world a better place.

INFPs do not like conflict and go to great lengths to avoid it. On the other hand, INFPs make very good mediators and are typically good at solving other people's conflicts, because they intuitively understand people's perspectives and feelings, and genuinely want to help them.

INFPs are flexible and laid-back, until one of their values is violated. In the face of their value system being threatened, INFPs can become aggressive defenders, fighting passionately for their cause. As a result of their high standards and perfectionism, they are usually hard on themselves, and don't give themselves enough credit.

INFPs appear frequently in social service professions, such as counseling or teaching. They are at their best in situations where they're working toward the public good, and in which they don't need to use hard logic. Some of the great, humanistic catalysts in the world have been INFPs.

The Keirsey Temperament Sorter Idealist-Healer

The Keirsey Temperament Sorter (KTS) question-naire is another personality assessment tool, developed by psychologist David W. Keirsey (see keirsey.com). It expands on the MBTI in assessing four temperaments and sixteen character types. Keirsey calls the highly sensitive INFP type the Idealist-Healer. In his book *Please Understand Me II*, the characteristics he lists for the Idealist-Healer offer a good description of HST, although he does not use the term "highly sensitive":

- Abstract in thought and speech
- Cooperative
- Introverted
- Appear reserved and shy
- Diplomatic
- Empathic
- Hunger for deep and meaningful relationships
- Value personal growth, authenticity, and integrity
- Internally deeply caring
- Deeply committed to the positive and the good
- A mission to bring peace to the world
- Strong personal morality

- Often make extraordinary sacrifices for someone or something they believe in
- Imagination and evolution are the goal
- Seek unity, feel divided inside
- Often had an unhappy childhood
- May have been raised in a practical, industrious, social family
- Didn't conform to parental expectations
- Often feel isolated, "like an alien"
- See themselves as ugly ducklings
- Rich fantasy world as a child, may have been discouraged or punished for this by parents
- Wish to please, try to hide their differences
- Believe and are told that their sensitivity is bad
- Drawn toward purity but continuously on the lookout for the wickedness they think lurks in them
- Self-sacrificing to an extreme, in atonement for their failings
- Keep this inner struggle hidden from others

According to Dr. Keirsey, the Idealist-Healer's intention is to foster:

- Profound awareness of sensations
- Loving goodness
- Mission to bring peace
- Deep sense of connection
- Vision of possibilities

- Idealism
- Healing
- High standards
- Intuition, empathy, perceptiveness
- Sense of unity, oneness
- Originality
- Deep sense of joy, beauty
- Love of nature

If you have been reading all of this and feeling "Yeah, that's me, all right," know that you are the help that is on the way, whether you are sensitive yourself or partnered, working with, interacting with, or the parent of someone who is sensitive. With Emotional Freedom Techniques (EFT), you can transform your life as a highly sensitive person (or introduce sensitive others to this transformative tool).

EFT is a wonderful tool for sensitive people. It can focus right in on the experiences that have hurt us so deeply, and dissolve both the pain and the beliefs we came to have about ourselves as a result. It can help us tap into the true blessing that each of us is in the world, and help us manifest this blessing in our everyday encounters.

In this next chapter, you will learn all you need to know about EFT to begin changing the way you think about and experience your sensitivity.

2

EFT's Basic Recipe

This chapter was prepared for readers of this book by EFT founder Gary Craig. It is adapted from his "million copy" EFT manual.

Welcome to EFT

The basic premise of EFT (Emotional Freedom Techniques) is that *the cause of all negative emotions is a disruption in the body's energy system.* I can't emphasize this concept enough. When our energy is flowing normally, without obstruction, we feel good in every way. When our energy becomes blocked, stagnant, or otherwise disrupted along one or more of the body's energy meridians, negative or damaging emotions can develop, along with all types of physical symptoms. This idea has been the centerpiece of Eastern medicine for thousands of years.

EFT is often called *emotional acupuncture* because it combines gentle tapping on key acupuncture points while focusing your thoughts on pain, unhappy memories, uncomfortable emotions, food cravings, or any other problem. Properly done, the underlying emotional factors that contribute to the problem are typically released along with the energy blocks.

Consider that:

- **EFT often works when nothing else will.**

- **EFT brings complete or partial relief in about 80 percent of the cases in which it's tried,** and in the hands of a skilled practitioner, its success rate can exceed 95 percent.

- **Sometimes the improvement is permanent,** while in other cases, the process needs to be continued. But even if symptoms return, they can usually be reduced or eliminated quickly and effectively just by repeating the procedure.

- **People are often astonished at the results they experience** because their belief systems have not yet adapted to this common-sense process. Physical, emotional, and performance issues are supposed to be much more difficult to resolve than simply by tapping with your fingertips on key acupuncture points.

- **The EFT basics are extremely easy to use.** Small children learn it quickly, and kids as young as eight or ten have no trouble teaching it to others. It's fully portable, requires no special equipment, and can be used at any time of the day or night and under any circumstances.

- **No drugs, surgeries, radiations, or other medical interventions** are involved in EFT. In fact, it's so different from conventional medicine that the medical profession often has difficulty explaining its results.

- **It doesn't seem to matter what the patient's blood tests or other diagnostic tests show.** Relief can occur with EFT no matter what the diagnosis. That's because EFT addresses a cause that tends to be outside the medical box.

- **This is not to say you should ignore your physician's advice.** On the contrary, I encourage you to consult with qualified health-care providers. Quite a few EFT practitioners are physicians, nurses, dentists, acupuncturists, chiropractors, massage therapists, psychologists, counselors, and other health-care professionals. As EFT becomes more widely known, it will become easier to find licensed health-care practitioners who are knowledgeable about EFT.

- **Using a few minutes of EFT will often improve your physical health.** When it doesn't, there is likely to be some underlying emotional issue that is creating chemicals and/or tension in your body, which interferes with the success.

- If that's the case, **EFT is ideal for collapsing and neutralizing emotional issues,** and it often does the job in minutes. EFT was originally designed to reduce the psychotherapy process from months or years down to minutes or, in complicated cases, a few sessions.

No technique or procedure works for everyone, but by all accounts, the vast majority of those who try EFT for a specific problem experience significant benefits. That's a stunning result and one that compares favorably with prescription drugs, surgical procedures, or medical treatments.

EFT is so new that it's still evolving. I encourage practitioners and newcomers alike to experiment, to try it on everything. It makes sense that if your energy is balanced, everything inside and around you benefits.

Whether you are new to EFT or already an experienced tapper, I am very pleased to share this information with you. I know without a doubt that EFT can help you take control of your health and happiness and that the instructions and recommendations given here can completely transform your life.

Defining the Problem

EFT sessions usually begin with a self-estimate of discomfort using a scale from 0 to 10. We call this the 0-to-10 intensity meter or intensity scale. The discomfort being measured can be physical, such as headache pain or a craving, or it can be an emotion such as fear, anxiety, depression, or anger.

It's a good idea to rate every problem before and after you apply EFT so that you can determine how much progress you're making. It's also important to assess your intensity as it exists now, rather than when the event or problem first occurred.

Intensity Meter

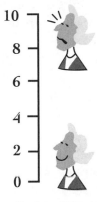

Don't worry if you find it difficult to select a specific number. Sometimes newbies (my affectionate term for EFT newcomers) get distracted by this part of the procedure and worry unnecessarily about whether it's a 5 or 6, or a 2 or 3. Using the 10-point scale becomes easy with practice. Just give yourself a number to get started and it will soon be automatic. It helps to remind yourself that there are no wrong answers here and that if you have trouble coming up with a specific number, a guess will work fine. It is simply a benchmark for comparison after you perform EFT.

For reference, jot the number down and add a few notes. For example, if you're focusing on a pain, think about where the pain is located, how it interferes with your range of motion, and whether it hurts more when you move to the left or right, stand or sit, and so forth.

Another way to indicate the intensity of pain or discomfort, which works well for children, is to move your hands wide apart for major pain and bring them close together for minor pain. Some children find it easier to express "big" and "small" with their hands rather than with a number scale.

The method you choose doesn't matter as long as it works for you. Keeping track of your pain's intensity before and after treatment is the easiest way to determine whether and how effectively the treatment is working.

The same scale works for feelings. First, focus on an event or memory or problem that has been bothering you. Now ask yourself how angry, anxious, depressed, or upset are you on a scale from 0-to-10. If it doesn't bother you at all, you're at 0. If you're at 10, that's the most it has ever been. Get in the habit of starting each tapping session with an intensity measurement and make a note of it.

Now, borrowing some pages from *The EFT Manual*, I'd like to introduce you to the Basic Recipe, the formula that is the foundation of this technique.

The Basic Recipe

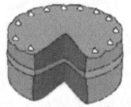

A recipe has certain ingredients that must be added in a certain order. If you are baking a cake, for example, you must use sugar instead of pepper and you must add the sugar *before* you put it in the oven. Otherwise, no cake.

Basic EFT is like a cake recipe. It has specific ingredients that go together in a specific way. Just as someone who is learning to cook will get the best results by following tried-and-true instructions, someone who is new to EFT will do well to learn the Basic Recipe. An accomplished chef will take a different approach, and so can you once you master the fundamentals.

What I'm going to show you here is a shortcut method of using EFT. It does not include everything that I teach in *The EFT Manual* or in the DVD training materials on the emofree.com website. Since first developing EFT, however, I have discovered that this shortcut method works very well almost all the time, so this is the primary method I now use, and so do most EFT practitioners. I encourage everyone to learn or at least know about the original version so that if you don't get the results you want, you can try the complete Basic Recipe. It is easy to learn and adds less than a minute to the procedure.

Focusing now on the shortcut method, here is what you need in order to start using EFT.

Ingredient #1: The Setup

To change analogies, applying the Basic Recipe is something like going bowling. In bowling, there is a machine that sets up the pins by picking them up and arranging them in perfect order at the end of the alley.

Once this setup is done, all you need to do is roll the ball down the alley to knock over the pins.

In a similar manner, the Basic Recipe has a beginning routine to set up your energy system as though it is a set of bowling pins. This routine (called the Setup) is vital to the whole process and prepares the energy system so that the rest of the Basic Recipe (the ball) can do its job.

Your energy system, of course, is not *really* a set of bowling pins. It is a set of subtle electric circuits. I present this bowling analogy only to give you a sense of the purpose of the Setup and the need to make sure your energy system is properly oriented before attempting to remove its disruptions.

Your energy system is subject to a form of electrical interference that can block the balancing effect of these tapping procedures. When present, this interfering blockage must be removed or the Basic Recipe will not work. Removing it is the job of the Setup.

Technically speaking, this interfering blockage takes the form of a *polarity reversal* within your energy system. This is different from the *energy disruptions* that cause your negative emotions.

Another analogy might help us here. Consider a flashlight or any other device that runs on batteries. If the batteries aren't there, the flashlight won't work. Equally important, the batteries must be installed properly. You've noticed, I'm sure, that batteries have + and − marks on them. Those marks indicate their polarity. If you line up those + and − marks according to the instructions, then the electricity flows normally and your flashlight works fine.

But what happens if you put the batteries in backward? Try it sometime. The flashlight will not work. It acts as if the batteries have been removed. That's what happens when polarity reversal is present in your energy system. It's like your batteries are in backward. I don't mean you stop working altogether, like turn "toes up" and die, but your progress becomes arrested in some areas.

This polarity reversal has an official name. It is called Psychological Reversal and it represents a fascinating discovery with wide-ranging applications in all areas of healing and personal performance. It is the reason why some diseases are chronic and respond very poorly to conventional treatments. It is also the reason why some people have such a difficult time losing weight or giving up addictive substances. It is, quite literally, the cause of self-sabotage.

Psychological Reversal is caused by self-defeating, negative thinking that often occurs subconsciously and thus outside of your awareness. On average, it is present, and thus hinders EFT, about 40 percent of the time. Some people have very little of it (this is rare), whereas others are beset by it most of the time (this also is rare). Most people fall somewhere in between these two extremes. Psychological Reversal doesn't create any feelings within you so you won't know if it is present or not. Even the most positive people (including yours truly) are subject to it.

When Psychological Reversal is present, it stops any attempt at healing, including EFT. Therefore it *must* be corrected if the rest of the Basic Recipe is going to work.

We correct for Psychological Reversal even though it might not be present. It only takes eight or ten seconds to do and, if it isn't present, no harm is done. If it *is* present, however, a major impediment to your success will be out of the way.

The Setup, which will correct Psychological Reversal, consists of two parts:

1. Saying an affirmation three times.
2. Simultaneously tap on the Karate Chop point.

The Affirmation

Since the cause of Psychological Reversal involves negative thinking, it should come as no surprise that the correction for it includes a neutralizing affirmation. Here is the formula for the affirmation:

> *Even though I have this* _____, *I deeply and completely accept myself.*

Fill in the blank with a brief description of the problem you want to address. Here are some examples:

Even though I have this <u>pain in my lower back</u>, I deeply and completely accept myself.

Even though I have this <u>fear of public speaking</u>, I deeply and completely accept myself.

Even though I have this <u>headache</u>, I deeply and completely accept myself.

Even though I have this <u>anger toward my father</u>, I deeply and completely accept myself.

Even though I have this <u>war memory</u>, I deeply and completely accept myself.

Even though I have this <u>stiffness in my neck</u>, I deeply and completely accept myself.

Even though I have <u>these nightmares</u>, I deeply and completely accept myself.

Even though I have this <u>craving for chocolate</u>, I deeply and completely accept myself.

Even though I have this <u>fear of snakes</u>, I deeply and completely accept myself.

Even though I have this <u>depression</u>, I deeply and completely accept myself.

This is only a partial list, of course, because the possible issues that are addressable by EFT are endless. You can also vary the acceptance phrase by saying:

I accept myself even though I have this _____ _____.

Even though I have this _____, *I deeply
and profoundly accept myself.*

Even though I have this _____, *I love and
forgive myself.*

*I love and accept myself even though I have this
_____.*

And there are more variations. Instead of saying, "I
completely and fully accept myself," you can simply say:

I'm okay.   *I'll be okay.*

I'll feel better soon.   *Everything's improving.*

Or something similar. This, by the way, is how we
use EFT with children. The phrase "I fully and completely accept myself" makes little sense to kids. Instead,
a child who is upset can say something like:

*Even though I flunked the math test, I'm a cool kid,
I'm okay.*

*Even though I lost my backpack and I'm mad at
myself, I'm still an awesome kid.*

All of these affirmations are correct because they follow the same general format. That is, they acknowledge
the problem and create self-acceptance despite the existence of the problem. That is what is necessary for the
affirmation to be effective. You can use any version, but
I suggest you start with the recommended one because it
is easy to memorize and has a good track record of getting
the job done.

Now here are some interesting points about the affirmation:

- It doesn't matter whether you believe the affirmation or not. Just say it.

- It is better to say it with feeling and emphasis, but saying it routinely will usually do the job.

- It is best to say it out loud, but if you are in a social situation where you prefer to mutter it under your breath or do it silently, then go ahead. It will probably be effective.

Tapping on the Karate Chop Point

To add to the effectiveness of the affirmation and clear Psychological Reversal, the Setup includes tapping the Karate Chop point while reciting the affirmation.

The Karate Chop Point

The Karate Chop point (abbreviated KC) is located at the center of the fleshy part of the outside of your hand (either hand) between the top of the wrist and the base of the baby finger, or stated differently, the part of your hand you would use to deliver a karate chop.

Tap the Karate Chop point solidly, using the fingertips of the index finger and middle finger (or all fingers) of the opposite hand. Although you can tap the Karate Chop point on either hand, it is usually most convenient to tap the point of the nondominant hand with the fingertips of the dominant hand. If you are right-handed, tap the Karate Chop point on your left hand with the fingertips of your right hand. If you are left-handed, tap the Karate Chop point on your right hand with the fingertips of your left hand.

Now that you understand the parts of the Setup, performing it is easy. You create a word or short phrase to fill in the blank in the affirmation and then simply repeat the affirmation, with emphasis, three times while continuously tapping the Karate Chop point.

That's it. After a few practice rounds, you should be able to perform the Setup in eight to ten seconds or so. Now, with the Setup properly performed, you are ready for the next ingredient in the Basic Recipe: the Sequence.

Ingredient #2: The Sequence

The Sequence is very simple in concept. It involves tapping at or near the end points of the major energy flows in the body (called "meridians" in Oriental medicine) and is the method by which the disruption in the energy system is balanced out. Before locating these points, however, you need a few tips on how to carry out the tapping process.

Tapping Tips

- You can tap with either hand, but it is usually more convenient to do so with your dominant hand (your right hand if you are right-handed or your left hand if you are left-handed).

- Tap with the fingertips of your index finger and middle finger. This covers a little larger area than just tapping with one fingertip and allows you to cover the tapping points more easily.

- Tap solidly but never so hard as to hurt or bruise yourself.

- Tap about seven times on each of the tapping points. I say *about* seven times because you will be repeating a "Reminder Phrase" (covered later) while tapping and it will be difficult to count at the same time. If you tap a few more than or a few less than seven times (five to nine, for example), that will be sufficient.

Most of the tapping points exist on either side of the body. It does not matter which side you use or if you switch sides during the Sequence. For example, you can tap under your right eye, and later in the Sequence, tap under your left arm.

The Points

Each energy meridian has two end points. For the purposes of the Basic Recipe, you need only tap on one end to balance out any disruptions that might exist in that meridian. These end points are near the surface of the body and are thus more readily accessed than other points along the meridians that may be more deeply buried. What follows are instructions on how to locate the end points of those meridians that are important to the Basic Recipe. Taken together and done in the order presented, they form the Sequence.

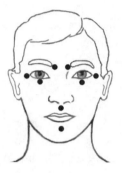

EB, SE, UE, UN, and Ch Points

1. **Eyebrow:** At the beginning of the eyebrow, just above and to one side of the nose. This point is abbreviated **EB** for beginning of the EyeBrow.

2. **Side of Eye:** On the bone bordering the outside corner of the eye. This point is abbreviated **SE** for Side of the Eye.

3. **Under Eye:** On the bone under an eye about one inch below your pupil. This point is abbreviated **UE** for Under the Eye.

4. **Under Nose:** On the small area between the bottom of your nose and the top of your upper lip. This point is abbreviated **UN** for Under the Nose.

5. **Chin:** Midway between the point of your chin and the bottom of your lower lip. Although it is not directly on the point of the chin, we call it the chin point because it is descriptive enough for people to understand easily. This point is abbreviated **Ch** for Chin.

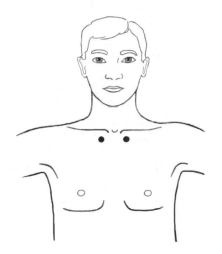

The Collarbone (CB) Points

6. **Collarbone:** The junction where the sternum (breastbone), collarbone, and first rib meet. Place your forefinger on the U-shaped notch at the top of the breastbone (where a man would knot his tie). Move down toward the navel one inch and then go to the left (or right) one to two inches. This point is abbreviated **CB** for CollarBone even though it is not on the collarbone (or clavicle) per se. It is at the beginning of the collarbone.

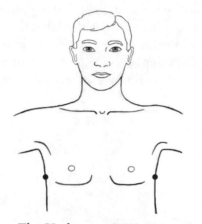

The Underarm (UA) Points

7. **Underarm:** On the side of the body, at a point even
    with the nipple (for men) or in the middle of the
    bra strap (for women). It is about four inches below
    the armpit. This point is abbreviated **UA** for Under
    the Arm.

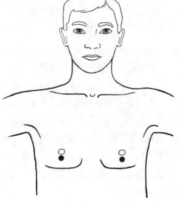

The Below Nipple (BN) Points

8. **Below Nipple:** For men, one inch below the nipple. For women, where the under skin of the breast meets the chest wall. This point is abbreviated **BN** for Below Nipple.

The abbreviations for these points are summarized below in the same order as given above.

1. **EB** = Beginning of the **E**ye**B**row

2. **SE** = **S**ide of the **E**ye

3. **UE** = **U**nder the **E**ye

4. **UN** = **U**nder the **N**ose

5. **Ch** = **Ch**in

6. **CB** = Beginning of the **C**ollar**B**one

7. **UA** = **U**nder the **A**rm

8. **BN** = **B**elow the **N**ipple

Notice that these tapping points proceed down the body. That is, each tapping point is below the one before it. That should make it a snap to memorize. A few trips through it and it should be yours forever.

The BN point has been added since I made my introductory EFT DVDs. It was originally left out because it's in an awkward place for women to tap while in social situations (restaurants, etc.) as well as in workshops. Even though the EFT results have been superb without it, I include it now for completeness.

The Reminder Phrase

Once memorized, the Basic Recipe becomes a lifetime friend. It can be applied to an almost endless list of emotional and physical problems, and it provides relief from most of them. However, there's one more concept we need to develop before we can apply the Basic Recipe to a given problem. It's called the Reminder Phrase.

When a football quarterback throws a pass, he aims it at a particular receiver. He doesn't just throw the ball in the air and hope someone will catch it. Likewise, the Basic Recipe needs to be aimed at a specific problem. Otherwise, it will bounce around aimlessly with little or no effect.

You "aim" the Basic Recipe by applying it while "tuned in" to the problem from which you want relief. This tells your system which problem needs to be the receiver.

Remember the EFT discovery statement, which says: *The cause of all negative emotions is a disruption in the body's energy system.* Negative emotions come about because you are tuned in to certain thoughts or circumstances that, in turn, disrupt your energy system. Otherwise, you function normally. Your fear of heights is not present, for example, while you are reading the comics section of the Sunday newspaper and therefore not tuned in to the problem.

Tuning in to a problem can be done simply by thinking about it. In fact, tuning in *means* thinking about it. Thinking about the problem will bring about the energy disruptions involved, which then and only then, can be balanced by applying the Basic Recipe. Without tuning in to the problem, thereby creating those energy disruptions, the Basic Recipe does nothing.

Tuning in is seemingly a very simple process. You merely think about the problem while applying the Basic Recipe. That's it, at least in theory. You might, however, find it a bit difficult to think about the problem while you are tapping. That's why I'm introducing a Reminder Phrase that you can repeat continually while performing the Basic Recipe.

The Reminder Phrase is simply a word or short phrase that describes the problem and that you repeat out loud each time you tap one of the points in the Sequence. In this way, you continually "remind" your system about the problem you are working on.

The best Reminder Phrase to use is usually identical to the phrase you insert in the affirmation for the Setup. For example, if you are working on a fear of public speaking, the Setup affirmation might go like this:

> *Even though I have this <u>fear of public speaking</u>, I deeply and completely accept myself.*

Within this affirmation, the underlined words, "fear of public speaking," are ideal for use as the Reminder Phrase.

I sometimes use a shorter version of this Reminder Phrase when in seminars such as those presented on my DVDs. I might, for example, use "public-speaking fear" or just "public speaking" instead of the somewhat longer version. That's just one of the shortcuts we have grown accustomed to after years of experience with these techniques. For your purposes, however, you can simply use identical words for both the Reminder Phrase and the affirmation phrase in the Setup. That way you will minimize the possibility of error.

Now here's an interesting point: I don't always have people repeat a Reminder Phrase. That's because I have discovered over time that simply stating the affirmation during the Setup is usually sufficient to tune in to the problem at hand. The subconscious mind usually locks on to the problem throughout the Basic Recipe even though tapping might seem distracting.

But this is not always true and, with extensive training and experience, one can recognize whether or not using the Reminder Phrase is necessary. As stated, it is not usually necessary, but when it is necessary, it is really necessary and must be used.

What's beautiful about EFT is that you don't need to have my experience in this regard. You don't have to be able to figure out whether or not the Reminder Phrase is necessary. You can just assume it is always necessary and thereby assure yourself of always being tuned in to the problem simply by repeating the Reminder Phrase as instructed. It does no harm to repeat the Reminder Phrase when it is not necessary, and it will serve as an invaluable tool when it is. We do many things in each round of the Basic Recipe that may not be necessary for a given problem. But when a particular part of the Basic Recipe is necessary, it is absolutely critical.

It does no harm to include everything, even what may be unnecessary, and it only takes one minute per round. This includes always repeating the Reminder Phrase each time you tap a point during the Sequence. It costs nothing to include it, not even time, because it can be repeated within the same time it takes to tap each energy point seven times.

This concept about the Reminder Phrase is an easy one. But just to be complete, here are a few samples of Reminder Phrases:

headache   *nightmares*

anger toward my father   *craving for chocolate*

war memory   *fear of snakes*

stiffness in my neck   *depression*

Test Your Results

At the end of one or two rounds of tapping all of the points in the Sequence, take another look at the problem you're working on. Measure it on the 0-to-10 intensity scale. Where is it now?

If it doesn't bother you at all any more and is at 0, congratulations. You're finished. No further tapping is required.

If you feel better, but the problem is still there, make a note of your new level of discomfort on the 0-to-10 intensity scale. For example, your headache pain may have gone from 9 to 4, or your anger toward your father might have moved from 8 to 5. Keeping track of the numbers helps you keep track of your progress.

If you are a practitioner, write down the problem your client is working on, the beginning intensity level, and the level after treatment. This helps both of you appreciate whatever improvement is being made, and it simplifies follow-up sessions.

If you're working on your own, write down every problem or issue you tap for, along with your results. After a few weeks of practice, you will be amazed at the number of issues you have cleared away, many of which you will have forgotten about by then.

Here's what to do if you or your client still have some discomfort after an initial round of tapping.

Subsequent Round Adjustments

When EFT tapping produces only partial relief, you will need to do one or more additional rounds. These subsequent rounds have to be adjusted slightly for best results. Here's why. One of the main reasons why the first round doesn't always completely eliminate a problem is because of the reemergence of Psychological Reversal, that interfering blockage that the Setup is designed to correct.

This time, Psychological Reversal shows up in a somewhat different form. Instead of blocking your progress altogether, it now blocks any *remaining* progress. You make some headway but become stopped on the way to complete relief because Psychological Reversal enters in a manner that keeps you from getting even better.

Since the subconscious mind tends to be very literal, subsequent rounds of the Basic Recipe need to address the fact that you are working on the *remaining problem.*

Accordingly, the affirmation contained within the Setup has to be adjusted, as does the Reminder Phrase.

> *Even though I **still** have **some** of this _____, I deeply and completely accept myself.*

Please note the emphasized words ("still" and "some") and how they change the thrust of the affirmation toward the remainder of the problem. It should be easy to make this adjustment and, after a little experience, you will fall into it quite naturally.

Study the affirmations that follow. They reflect adjustments to the original affirmations shown earlier in this section.

> *Even though I **still** have **some** of this <u>fear of public speaking</u>, I deeply and completely accept myself.*

> *Even though I **still** have **some** of this <u>headache</u>, I deeply and completely accept myself.*

> *Even though I **still** have **some** of this <u>anger toward my father</u>, I deeply and completely accept myself.*

> *Even though I **still** have **some** of this <u>war memory</u>, I deeply and completely accept myself.*

> *Even though I **still** have **some** of this <u>stiffness in my neck</u>, I deeply and completely accept myself.*

> *Even though I **still** have **some** of these <u>nightmares</u>, I deeply and completely accept myself.*

> *Even though I **still** have **some** of this <u>craving for chocolate</u>, I deeply and completely accept myself.*

> *Even though I **still** have **some** of this <u>fear of snakes</u>, I deeply and completely accept myself.*

*Even though I **still** have **some** of this <u>depression</u>, I deeply and completely accept myself.*

The Reminder Phrase is also easily adjusted. Just put the word "remaining" before the previously used phrase. Here, as examples, are the previous Reminder Phrases:

> **remaining** *headache*
>
> **remaining** *nightmares*
>
> **remaining** *anger toward my father*
>
> **remaining** *craving for chocolate*
>
> **remaining** *war memory*
>
> **remaining** *fear of snakes*
>
> **remaining** *stiffness in my neck*
>
> **remaining** *depression*

If your symptom or condition disappears but then returns, simply repeat EFT's Basic Recipe and the "remaining" Reminder Phrase as described.

Ingredient #3: The 9 Gamut Procedure

The 9 Gamut Procedure is, perhaps, the most bizarre looking process within EFT. Its purpose is to fine-tune the brain and it does so via some eye movements and some humming and counting. Through connecting nerves, certain parts of the brain are stimulated when the eyes are moved. Likewise the right side of the brain (the creative side) is engaged when you hum a song and the left side (the digital side) is engaged when you count.

The 9 Gamut Procedure is a ten-second process in which you perform nine brain-stimulating actions while continuously tapping on one of the body's energy points, the Gamut point. It has been found, after years of experience, that this routine can add efficiency to EFT and hasten your progress toward emotional freedom, especially when sandwiched between two trips through the Sequence.

One way to help memorize the Basic Recipe is to look at it as though it iss a ham sandwich. The Setup is the preparation for the ham sandwich and the sandwich itself consists of two slices of bread (the Sequence) with the ham, or middle portion, as the 9 Gamut Procedure.

The Gamut Point

To do the 9 Gamut Procedure, you must first locate the Gamut point. It is on the back of either hand, half an inch toward the wrist from the point between the knuckles at the base of the ring finger and the little finger. If you draw an imaginary line between the knuckles at the base of the ring finger and little finger and consider that line to be the base of an equilateral triangle whose other sides converge to a point (apex) in the direction of the wrist, then the Gamut point would be located at the apex of the triangle.

The Gamut Point

Next, you must perform nine different actions while tapping the Gamut point continuously. These nine Gamut actions are:

1. Close your eyes.

2. Open your eyes.

3. Look down hard right while holding your head steady.

4. Look down hard left while holding your head steady.

5. Roll your eyes in a circle as though your nose is at the center of a clock and you are trying to see all the numbers in order. Hold your head steady.

6. Roll your eyes in a circle in the reverse direction. Hold your head steady.

7. Hum two seconds of a song (I usually suggest "Happy Birthday").

8. Count rapidly from 1 to 5.

9. Hum two seconds of a song again.

Note that these nine actions are presented in a certain order. I suggest that you memorize them in the order given. You can mix the order up if you wish, however, as long as you do all nine of them and perform the last three together as a unit. That is, you hum for two seconds, then count, then hum the song again, in that order. Years of experience have proven this to be important.

Note that these nine actions are presented in a certain order. I suggest that you memorize them in the order given. You can mix the order up if you wish, however, as long as you do all nine of them and perform the last three together as a unit. That is, you hum for two seconds, then count, then hum the song again, in that order. Years of experience have proven this to be important.

Note also that for some people humming "Happy Birthday" causes resistance because it brings up memories of unhappy birthdays. In this case, you can either use EFT on those unhappy memories and resolve them or side-step this issue for now by humming some other song.

Tapping with and for Others

I should add that EFT can be done by you on yourself, by another person on you, and by you on another person. All of these approaches to EFT tapping work equally well. If you watch the EFT training DVDs, you will see that in seminars and workshops, I routinely tap on the EFT points of the people I work with onstage. The technique of tapping on another person makes it easy for parents to apply EFT to their infants and small children and for anyone to apply EFT to those who for various reasons are not able to tap on or for themselves.

Introducing Aspects

Aspects are the various pieces of an emotional issue that may show up during an EFT session. Fortunately, they can be handled easily.

Let's say, for example, that you have a fear of spiders that you would like to put behind you. If there is no spider present to cause you any emotional intensity, then close your eyes and imagine seeing a spider, or imagine a past time when a spider scared you. Assess your intensity on a scale of 0 to 10 as it exists now while you think about it. If you estimate it at 7, for example, then you have a benchmark against which to measure your progress.

Now do one round of the Basic Recipe and imagine the spider again. If you can find no trace whatsoever of your previous emotional intensity, then you are finished. If, on the other hand, you go to, let's say, 4 on the scale, then you need to perform subsequent rounds until your intensity falls to 0.

You might wonder at this point whether getting to zero while just thinking about a spider will hold up when you actually confront a real spider. The answer is usually yes! In most cases, the energy disruptions that occur while thinking about the spider are the same as those when you are in the presence of a real spider. That's why the original energy balancing tends to hold in real circumstances.

The exception to this is when some new aspect of the problem comes up in the real situation that wasn't there when you were just thinking about it. For example, you may have been thinking about a stationary spider. If movement is an important aspect of your fear and if it was absent from your thinking when you did the original EFT rounds, then that part of the fear will arise when you see a moving spider.

This is a reasonably common occurrence and it doesn't mean that EFT didn't work. It simply means there is more to do. Just apply the Basic Recipe to the new aspect (moving spider) until your emotional response falls to zero on the scale. Once all aspects have been eliminated, your phobic response to spiders should be history and you can be perfectly calm around them.

Someone who's haunted by a traffic accident might be affected by memories of oncoming headlights, anger toward the other driver, the sound of screeching brakes, or the sight of window glass shattering. A war trauma can have aspects such as the sight of blood, the look in a comrade's eyes before he dies, the sound of a hand grenade, or the memory of an explosion or gunfire. A rape experience can have aspects such as the smell of the assailant's breath, the sound of his voice, the impact of a fist, or the penetration. A fear of public speaking can have aspects such as the sight of a microphone, the onlooking eyes of the audience, or a memory of being ridiculed as a child.

Another thing to recognize is that an aspect can also be an emotion. Some clients report that the anger they had regarding a given event has shifted to sadness. Pick up on these clues. These different emotional aspects are taking you deeper into the problem. They are opportunities for greater healing and present you with great possibilities for mastering your craft.

The notion of aspects is an important one in EFT. As in the previous examples, some problems have many pieces or aspects to them and the problem will not be completely relieved until all of them are addressed. Actually, each of these aspects qualifies as a separate problem even though they seem to be all lumped together. The fear of a stationary spider and the fear of a moving spider, for example, would seem to be lumped together. In fact, they are separate problems that need to be addressed separately by EFT.

Different aspects are possible with just about any problem you want to address with EFT. Each aspect may be a separate problem that needs to be addressed individually before complete relief is obtained.

Please understand that where several aspects of an emotional problem are present, you may not notice any relief until all aspects are reduced to zero by the Basic Recipe. This becomes very clear when you consider different aspects of physical healing. If, for example, you have a simultaneous headache, toothache, and stomachache, you will not feel healthy until all three are gone. The pain may seem to shift but it is, nonetheless, still pain. So it is with emotional issues that contain different aspects. Even if you have taken care of one or more aspects, you may not experience relief until you hav e dealt with all of the problem's aspects.

Experienced EFTers often compare this procedure to peeling an onion. You get rid of one layer only to discover another. When a problem has many layers or aspects, neutralizing them with EFT can seem like a daunting project. But considering how quickly those layers can be dealt with and how beneficial the results are, the project is more exciting than intimidating. And the rewards are priceless.

Core Issues

By far the fastest way to resolve a complex issue or clear up symptoms that resist treatment is to discover the problem's *core issue*. Core issues are fundamental emotional imbalances, usually related to traumatic events.

There are many ways to approach core issues. In some cases, they are obvious to the person. When asked about when a problem started or what might be contributing to it, the reply is immediate. "I'll bet it has something to do with my husband's heart attack last fall." "I turn to food whenever I think about my wife's affair, and my overeating is out of control." "Ever since my business failed, my back has been killing me."

But many times, core issues are hidden from view. This is because the subconscious mind is a clever protector of secrets, including those that we hide from ourselves. In some cases, our subconscious minds hide secrets that are truly awful. But most of them, when looked at objectively, don't amount to much.

Examples: The reason Tom can't give a presentation at work is because his fourth grade teacher embarrassed him in front of the class. The reason Ann can't lose weight is because, when she was eight years old, her mother told her she would always be too fat to wear a swimsuit. The reason John can't propose to Marie is because his older sister always told him that he was such a loser, no one would ever marry him. The reason Susan can't take an elevator is because when she was trapped in an elevator for five minutes several years ago, the friend who was with her started screaming.

As long as they hold an emotional charge, these secrets are powerful enough to shape a person's life, but as soon as they are uncovered and neutralized with EFT, core issues like these lose their power and become insignificant old memories.

This feature of EFT never ceases to amaze me. Again and again I've worked with people while they dealt with incredibly painful memories, memories that controlled their lives and dictated where they would live, what career they would follow, what friends they would have, and everything else. Suddenly, after a few rounds of EFT tapping, they are completely transformed and no longer frightened, anxious, or afraid of old events. Instead, they're able to describe these events as easily as if they were talking about the weather. As soon as old events and old memories lose their emotional charge, they lose their place of power in the subconscious mind.

Be Specific

If you want fast, impressive results with EFT, be specific. Vague statements generate vague outcomes. The biggest mistake made by newcomers is using EFT on issues that are too global. Global problems are broad and hazy. They aren't well defined. Even with perseverance, which can almost always make a difference, global statements are less likely to produce results than specific statements about specific events.

I have been beating the drum for many years about being specific with EFT, urging EFTers to break emotional issues into the events that underlie them. When we do this, we address true causes and not just symptoms. Though there is a skill to doing this, those who take this approach have watched their success rates climb impressively. They are also doing deeper, more meaningful work.

I have found, and demonstrated consistently, that applying EFT to the smallest component of a bothersome memory almost always works. This idea has the potential to substantially improve EFT's success rate and pave the way for healing in areas previously thought difficult or impossible. Many newcomers to EFT present their emotional issues in very global terms. They say things like:

I feel abandoned.	*I'm always anxious.*
I was an abused child.	*I hate my father.*
I have low self-esteem.	*I can't do anything right.*
I'm depressed.	*I feel overwhelmed.*

To them, that is the problem and that is what they want EFT to fix. But, despite the person's perception, that is not the problem at all. Those feelings are merely symptoms of the problem. The real problem is the unresolved specific events, memories, and emotions that caused the larger issue. How can one feel abandoned or abused, for example, unless specific events occurred in one's life to cause those feelings? The feelings didn't just appear out of the ether. They must have had a cause.

If we consider the larger issue (such as abandonment) to be a tabletop, then the table's legs represent specific events that support the table (e.g., "My mother died when I was seven," "My father walked out on us when I was eleven," or "I got lost on a hiking trip in the Sierra mountains"). Obviously, if we reduce an issue to the specific events supporting it and then collapse its table legs, the tabletop will fall for lack of support. In this way, we address the true causes (specific events and emotions linked to them) rather than just symptoms.

Unfortunately, many EFT practitioners still apply EFT to the tabletop and not the supporting table legs. Thus they might start with:

Even though I have this feeling of abandonment...

Being too global like this is the number-one error made by new EFTers and some seasoned ones, too. Interestingly, this approach will sometimes get results, but it is not nearly as thorough or precise as going for the supporting table legs first. Also, because this global approach lacks precision, those using it are more likely to report that their issues "come back." What "comes back," of course, are unresolved aspects (table legs) that were not previously addressed.

In addition, approaching an issue in a vague or global manner creates an environment in which the person's attention shifts from event to event. You can be much more accurate and achieve greater success if you reduce those global issues (tabletops) to the specific events (table legs) that cause them. Examples for the global issue of "I feel abandoned" could include:

The time my mother left me in the shopping mall when I was in second grade.

The time my father told me to leave home when I was twelve.

The time my third-grade teacher gave me that "I don't care about you" look.

These specific events are much easier to deal with than the global issues they created. If you deal with them one at a time without letting your attention shift, it will be easy to clear them. And by clearing the emotions stored in these small specific events, you automatically repair the larger global issue.

To help you find specific events to tap on, ask yourself questions like: *When did this problem start? What was I doing at the time? What was going on in my life? What does this remind me of?*

The Watch the Movie and Tell the Story Techniques

In our search for core issues, we often use the Watch the Movie and Tell the Story techniques. In both methods, you review a past event while tapping to reduce its emotional charge. The difference between the two is that in the Movie Technique, you watch events unfold in your mind, as though you're watching a movie, while in the Story Technique, you describe the events aloud.

The "plot" of the movie or story is usually very short. If not, reduce the length down to one or two emotional crescendos because that sets up the target for EFT's aim. If jumping straight to the key event is too painful, however, the movie or story can begin a few minutes before the first emotional crescendo. The event may have hurt, but its retelling doesn't have to.

Unlike psychotherapy techniques that require clients to relive unpleasant past events in excruciating detail, EFT's approach is gentle and flexible. You watch the movie or tell the story until you reach a point that feels uncomfortable. Instead of forcing yourself to push on, step back and tap until the emotional intensity fades.

When you feel comfortable again, resume the movie or story. When feelings arise again, take a step back and tap. In this simple two-steps-forward and one-step-back process, you can often revisit any specific memory and completely neutralize its emotional impact in minutes.

Our bodies store traumas, and our mental movies are keys that unlock the emotions stored with those traumas. Because EFT tapping reduces the emotional charge attached to past events, it transforms the traumas, memories, energy blocks, targeted body parts, and emotions that were previously locked together. With the emotional charge gone, the traumas become normal memories, the connections disappear, and the pain once associated with them vanishes as well.

Secondary Gain

"Secondary gain" is a psychiatric term denoting that the person has a hidden or unconscious reason for holding onto an undesirable condition. The term applies to a wide variety of issues. An example is a chronic pain case in which the patient will lose certain benefits if he or she gets well, such as attention from others, monetary compensation for disability, or the ability to keep denying the original cause of the pain.

In metaphysics, the term "secondary gain" helps explain why we seem to run into barriers when it comes to manifesting our good. This occurs when we put a great deal of energy into visualizing, affirming, and treating for a new level of good and either it doesn't happen or the situation actually gets worse. The subconscious mind feels more secure in the disadvantaged state than in going for improvement. So your conscious mind might be saying:

I sincerely want to get over this problem.

while your subconscious mind says:

I don't want to get over this problem because…

I can't ever get over this problem because…

It would be dangerous for me to get over this problem…

I can't afford to get over this problem…

What benefits do you receive from your problem? Does keeping the problem feel safe? Does releasing it feel dangerous? Does keeping the problem generate sympathy from others that you won't receive if you're well? Does keeping the problem allow you to avoid unpleasant situations? Does keeping the problem give you financial rewards that you won't receive if you get well? Do you feel you don't deserve to get over the problem? Do you fear that if you get better, something bad will happen?

I don't want to give up my problem because…

…if I get completely well, I'll lose my disability payments and I'll have to get a job, and who knows how long that will take, and I've been unemployed for so long that I wouldn't know where to go or what to do, and the whole idea is just too stressful.

…if I get completely well, I'll have to move.

…my problem is such an important part of my identity that I won't know who I'll be if it goes away.

...it's just too difficult.

Some short, effective Setup Phrases that help neutralize the benefits of secondary gain include:

> *Even though I prefer to keep my problem because _____, I deeply and completely accept myself.*
>
> *Even though part of me wants to stay sick, disabled, and incapacitated, I fully and completely accept myself.*
>
> *Even though I like having this problem and intend to keep it and no one can make me give it up, so there, I nevertheless love and accept myself, I forgive and bless myself, I forgive the part of me that keeps holding onto it, and I choose to facilitate the rapid healing of my body and all my emotions by releasing all my energy blocks beginning right now.*

Of course, these statements are magnets for everything in your subconscious that believes them, but all of these can be treated with EFT. Just notice what comes into your mind and keep tapping.

The Personal Peace Procedure

In my online tutorial, I describe the Personal Peace Procedure, which is an easy exercise that can be worked on whenever you practice EFT. Try it now. The sooner you start, the sooner you'll experience true personal peace.

1. **Make a list.** On a blank sheet of paper, make a list of every bothersome specific event you can remember. If you don't find at least fifty, you are either going at this halfheartedly or you have been living on some other planet. Many people find hundreds.

2. **List everything.** While making your list, you may find that some events don't seem to cause you any current discomfort. That's okay. List them anyway. The mere fact that you remember them suggests a need for resolution.

3. **Give each event a title** as though it is a mini-movie. Examples: Dad hit me in the kitchen; I stole Suzie's sandwich; I almost slipped and fell into the Grand Canyon; My third grade class ridiculed me when I gave that speech; Mom locked me in a closet for two days; Mrs. Adams told me I was stupid.

4. **Tap for the big ones.** When the list is complete, pick out the biggest redwoods in your negative forest (the ones closest to a 10 on the intensity scale) and apply EFT to each one of them until you either laugh about it or just can't think about it anymore. Be sure to notice any aspects that come up and consider them separate trees in your negative forest. Apply EFT to them accordingly. Be sure to keep after each event until it is resolved down to 0 onnn the scale. After the biggest redwoods are removed, look for the next-biggest, and so on.

5. **Work on at least one movie (preferably three) per day for three months.** It takes only minutes per day. At this rate, you will have resolved 90 to 270 specific events in three months. Then notice how your body feels better. Note, too, how your threshold for getting upset is much lower. Note how your relationships are better and how many of your therapy-type issues just don't seem to be there anymore. Revisit some

of those specific events and notice how those previously intense incidents have faded into nothingness. Note any improvements in your life. I ask you to consciously notice these things because, unless you do, the quality healing you will have undergone may be so subtle that you don't notice it. You may even dismiss it by saying, "Oh well, it was never much of a problem anyway." This happens repeatedly with EFT and thus I bring it to your awareness.

6. **If necessary, see your physician.** If you are taking prescription medications, you might feel the need to discontinue them. Please do so *only* under the supervision of a qualified physician.

It is my hope that the Personal Peace Procedure will become a worldwide routine. A few minutes per day will make a monumental difference in school performance, relationships, health, and our quality of life. But these are meaningless words unless you put the idea into practice. As my good friend Howard Wight writes, "If you are ultimately going to do something important that will make a real difference, do it now."

3

Start Tapping
Right Now!

Let's begin! Here is how a tapping routine might go for you as a highly sensitive person, encountering the stresses of a normal day.

Think of a small incident that happened recently at work, in your family, or with an acquaintance, something that bothered you and that you are finding hard to let go of. Think of what really bothered you about the incident. Was it the look on the person's face? The tone of the person's voice? What did you think that meant about you? Write down your responses to these questions and anything else about the incident that occurs to you.

Give the event a title. Examples: "She said _____ and it hurt my feelings," or "He gave me that look and I felt_____," or "That was the last straw—I just can't get all this done."

Rate the intensity of the feelings you have about it on the 0-to-10 intensity scale.

1. EFT Setup Phrases

Put the phrase that contains what bothered you most into a Setup statement like these (change the words to fit your own situation):

Even though that happened, and I am so sensitive to things like this so it made me feel _____, I accept myself anyway.

Even though the look on his/her face made me think _____, I love and accept myself anyway. I was doing the best I could.

Even though I can't seem to let go of all my feelings about this—I am too sensitive—I love and accept myself anyway, and I am choosing to feel as good as I can right now.

While tapping the Karate Chop point on either hand, repeat your phrase out loud.

2. Tap Through the Points

Now, tap through the points, using your title and your feelings:

Eyebrow: *She/he said_____.* (use your title in the blanks)

Side of Eye: *She said_____.*

Under Eye: *She said_____.*

Under Nose: *She said_____.*

Chin: *I feel hurt and misunderstood.*

Collarbone: *It is really my fault. What is wrong with me? I get overwhelmed so easily.*

Under Arm: *I feel sad and angry and all alone.*

Top of Head: *She said_____ and that made me think _____.*

Note: I don't use the Below Nipple point and I have my clients tap on the top of the head at the end of the tapping sequence. The results are the same.

3. Check-in

Replay your memory of the incident. Notice what is different about your response. Check your 0-to-10 intensity level.

You might do another round with the same Setup phrases as previously, and tapping on the points this way:

Eyebrow: *I feel so bad. I am too sensitive! Everyone always said that.*

Side of Eye: *Why can't I just let this roll off my back?*

Under Eye: *What he/she did was wrong.*

Under Nose: *I don't like being treated that way.*

Chin: *That really hurt my feelings*

Collarbone: *I shouldn't be so upset about this! What is wrong with me?*

Under Arm: *It was my fault. I have to tough it out and soldier on.*

Head: *Maybe part of me doesn't want to let go of this issue.*

Now do another round, and experiment with creative ways to rephrase or reframe the story you have been telling yourself about this incident:

Even though that happened, I have decided to accept myself anyway. I wouldn't give up my sensitivity—it gives my life richness and meaning.

Even though I like to feel resentful sometimes, I accept who I am and how I feel.

Even though that happened, I choose to feel as good as I can right now.

Try some phrases and questions that gently and respectfully begin to shift your way of thinking about this incident, what it meant to you, and how your sensitive temperament responded. Imagine that you are taking the perspective of a loving wise advisor:

Eyebrow: *Is there a different way I could be thinking about this?*

Side of Eye: *I could let go of this resentment if I chose to.*

Under Eye: *Maybe I have more choices about my feelings.*

Under Nose: *I could always go back to this negative feeling later.*

Chin: *What if I am right to feel this way? What if I decided to feel good right now?*

Collarbone: *I appreciate all of my feelings and I appreciate that I care so deeply.*

Under Arm: *I choose to feel relieved and peaceful. We were both doing the best we could.*

Head: *I appreciate the relief and the joy I am tapping into.*

Check in again. Notice what feelings and thoughts remain. Check your intensity level. If you need to, go ahead and do some more rounds of tapping for "This remaining feeling…"

4. Point Yourself in a Healing Direction

For a highly sensitive person, it is very important to take this change work beyond just dissolving the negative feelings about the incident. HST thinking tends to go deeper and be more expansive than most people's thinking. You can use EFT to invite yourself into the next step, spiritually and philosophically. Let your inner spirit open into considering some deeper truths about you as you tap:

Even though that happened, I love and accept myself anyway. I honor myself for how hard that was.

Even though I like to feel resentful sometimes, I accept who I am and how I feel. Maybe feeling hurt and resentful is a way I use to feel powerful.

Even though that happened, I choose to feel as good as I can right now, and I ask for heartfelt wisdom to bring healing to this. I wonder if there are better and more effective ways to feel powerful.

Then tap on the following phrases as you complete one more round:

I love knowing that I deserve better.

I choose to believe in myself and value my sensitive temperament.

I appreciate that harmony is so important to me.

I love appreciating myself.

I'm grateful for this opportunity to rethink this incident.

I appreciate exactly who I am — being so sensitive could be a gift.

I appreciate all the lessons I have learned.

I am so grateful for all the goodness in my life.

I am glad to have such a fine-tuned guidance system in my feelings.

Check in again, and notice how you feel and think about that incident now.

If you do EFT for just a few minutes on all the little incidents that come up in a day, you will find your life changing dramatically. The sensitivity that seemed like a burden and a flaw before will begin to appear as the gift it is — a precise guidance system that lets you know right away when you are getting off the track of your deepest truth.

Nicole: Getting HST Relief and Insights from EFT

Nicole, a sophomore in college, came in to my office with a bright smile, but soon it became apparent that she was suffering from feeling overwhelmed in all the important areas of her life: self-image, school, friends, relationships, and family. She told me that all her life she had been told that she "gets too upset." I introduced her to the concept of the highly sensitive person. It helped her to know that there is not something wrong with her, though it is hard for her to remember that. She continually returned to the thought that there must be something wrong with her. She kept apologizing for it.

Nicole started out by saying she has been dieting, and she was so mad at herself about food. She was either eating or starving herself. Just that week she had had a realization: Whenever a troubling thought or feeling comes up, she reaches for something to eat to deflect her attention away from her discomfort.

I told her how brilliant that was of her to make that connection. So many people go through their entire lives medicating themselves in this way with food, sex, work, drugs, or smoking, and they don't ever make the connection. Nicole was bemused to be called brilliant when she was describing her terrible habits, but she took it in.

There were so many issues that Nicole felt mired in that we began to work with EFT on just feeling overwhelmed in general. She burst into tears, sobbing for a moment, but also apologizing and trying to control herself because she does not usually express how she really feels to anyone (not even to herself). So we just tapped up and down the points for a few minutes, and I came over to sit beside her to tap on her fingers while she cried and talked a bit.

Then we tapped on her history of being told that she "gets too upset." I asked her how it felt in her body to be so sensitive. Where did she feel it? She said she felt it in her chest—a heavy feeling weighing on her chest.

Often when people can't at first describe how something feels, I ask questions such as: Is it warmer or cooler?

Is it heavier or lighter? Is it lighter or darker? Is there a color, or not? Is it a moving feeling or a still feeling? Where do you feel it in your body? People can almost always answer these questions.

We tapped about this heavy feeling, and some specific incidents when she felt it.

I asked her to describe the feeling. Paradoxically, she said that even though the "too sensitive feeling" was heavy on her chest, inside her it felt as if she were too light.

I talked a bit about the fact that many people overeat and gain weight because they unconsciously feel this sense of "too-lightness," and they want to add a sense of presence, even an intimidating presence. Consciously or unconsciously, they overeat to increase their "heaviness" in the world. Nicole was intrigued with this idea.

I also told her about orthorexia, which is a kind of reverse of overeating. Orthorexia is an obsession with eating healthy food. It is related to anorexia, though a different eating disorder. Whereas an anorexic wants to lose weight, an orthorexic wants to feel pure, healthy, and natural. In a way, orthorexia is a rejection of the body, a wanting to be "lighter," even in a (distorted) spiritual sense. I say "distorted" spiritual sense, because I believe that as human beings we are like distilled spiritual energy, literally "denser" spirit. So when Nicole described the too-sensitive feeling as heavier, I heard her saying that she was experiencing her own spiritual presence on the earth. Noticing that she actually felt present in the world was unfamiliar to her, and a little scary.

Just like low self-esteem, a sense of spiritual presence is an "inside job" of beliefs, self-image, perspectives, and sense of purpose. Spiritual presence is a sense of feeling full, full of one's Self, a fulfilling. (There is lots of creative EFT languaging possible here.)

We tapped for filling herself deeply with this sensation. Next I invited her to imagine having more of a sense of her spiritual presence in those situations where in the past she had felt "too sensitive," as if there were something wrong with her. We included all of this positive languaging in our rounds of tapping.

Tapping with Nicole

Nicole and I had been meeting regularly. Her life situation and family history were complex, and there were many directions we could have taken in this session. We chose to tap on being "so mad at myself about food." We used that phrase to open the EFT Setup statement. Her feelings were anger, upset, and sadness. She rated the intensity of her feelings about this issue at an 8 on the 0–10 scale.

1. Nicole's Setup Phrases

Even though I am so mad at myself about food I accept myself anyway.

Even though I am so mad at myself about food, I love and accept myself anyway. I was doing the best I could.

Even though I can't seem to let go of all my feelings about this—I am so mad at myself about food! Why can't I control myself? I know better! Still, I love and accept myself anyway, and I am choosing to feel as good as I can right now.

While tapping the Karate Chop point, she repeated these phrases out loud.

2. Tapping Through the Points

Then we tapped through the points, using her title and her feelings:

Eyebrow: *I am so mad at myself about food.*

Side of Eye: *I am so mad at myself about food.*

Under Eye: *I am so mad at myself about food.*

Under Nose: *I am so mad at myself about food.*

Chin: *When I am upset, I reach for food.*

Collarbone: *What is wrong with me? I get overwhelmed so easily.*

Under Arm: *I feel sad and angry and all alone.*

Head: *I am either eating or starving myself.*

3. Check-in

We replayed Nicole's memory of the most recent incident of being upset and reaching for something to eat. Her intensity level had gone down to 6. She felt more relaxed though still upset. We did another round with the same Setup phrases as previously, tapping on the points this way:

Eyebrow: *I get too upset. I am too sensitive! Everyone always said that.*

Side of Eye: *Why can't I just let this roll off my back?*

Under Eye: *I should be able to deal with my feelings without food.*

Under Nose: *But I feel so overwhelmed. I need comfort.*

Chin: *There is no one I can talk to who would understand me. I never share what I really feel. I feel so sad about that.*

Collarbone: *I shouldn't be so upset about this! What is wrong with me?*

Under Arm: *I am still so mad at myself about food.*

Head: *Maybe part of me doesn't want to let go of this — what would I do to feel better without it? Food is my friend!*

We did another round, experimenting with creative ways to rephrase or reframe the story she had been telling herself about this problem.

Even though I eat when I get upset, I have decided to accept myself anyway. I am open to considering this more deeply.

Even though I feel the too-sensitive feeling in my chest as a heavy feeling and I feel too light on the inside, I accept who I am and how I feel. Maybe there is something positive about this.

Even though I feel too light and vulnerable inside, I choose to feel as good as I can right now. What if some part of me is trying to make me feel safer by feeling heavier? Maybe I can find a way that works better than eating to help me feel stronger and more solid inside.

I invited Nicole to try out some phrases and questions that would gently and respectfully begin to shift her thinking about this issue, what it meant to and for her, and how her sensitive temperament responded.

Eyebrow: *Is there a different way I could be thinking about this?*

Side of Eye: *I could let go of feeling so bad about myself if I chose to.*

Under Eye: *Maybe I have more choices about my feelings.*

Under Nose: *Maybe I could use that strong feeling on the inside of me to fill up where I feel too light.*

Chin: *What if I am OK? What if it is a good thing to be sensitive? What if I decided to feel good inside right now?*

Collarbone: *I appreciate all of my feelings and I appreciate that I care so deeply.*

Under Arm: *I choose to feel strong and warm inside. I can feel heavy inside in a good way, in a spiritually present way. Then that part of me that is running the eating behaviors doesn't have to make me heavy in my body to feel safe and less vulnerable.*

Head: *I appreciate the relief and the joy I am tapping into.*

When we checked in again, Nicole was feeling markedly better, more relaxed, and easier with herself. She was no longer angry with herself. Now she could see that a part of her had been trying to take care of her when she got overwhelmed and upset, and the only tool it had was food.

4. Pointing Nicole in a Healing Direction

What follows in this session with Nicole is a good example of how to use EFT to deepen your perspective on what is possible for you. As the practitioner (you can do this for yourself if you are tapping on your own issues), I invited Nicole to take a deeper look at her difficulties around food. Once I could feel that "taking care of" part of her emerging, I wanted her to learn how to apply it to herself. We are so used to meeting the needs and expectations of other people in our lives that we don't learn how to take care of ourselves. What seems to happen is that we take care of others, trying to get their approval; and when it doesn't come, we decide that there must be "something wrong with me." I wanted Nicole to appreciate the caretaker in her from another angle: by "deeply and completely loving and accepting" herself by caring about how she felt.

We tapped:

Even though I get overwhelmed and upset easily, I love and accept myself anyway. I honor myself for how hard it is to be a sensitive person in this culture.

Even though I realize now that I felt too light inside, and too easily hurt, I accept who I am and how I feel. Maybe I have been overeating to increase my "heaviness" in the world, and now that I understand this, I can find better and more effective ways to stand up for myself.

Even though I was mad at myself about food, I understand it all better now, and I ask for heartfelt wisdom to bring healing to this old way of thinking. I want to tell a new story about myself!

We tapped on the points with more phrases to complete one more round:

I love knowing that I deserve better.

I choose to believe in myself and value my sensitive temperament.

I appreciate that harmony is so important to me.

I love appreciating myself.

I'm grateful for this opportunity to rethink this incident.

I appreciate exactly who I am—being so sensitive could be a gift.

I appreciate all the lessons I have learned.

I am so grateful for all the goodness in my life.

I am glad to have such a fine-tuned guidance system in my feelings.

I love feeling fulfilled, just by being myself.

I asked Nicole to go inside again and check in again about those times that she ate when she felt upset and overwhelmed. When she opened her eyes, she said, "Well, when I see it this way, there really isn't any problem!"

I asked her to say the phrase "I'm so mad at myself about food." There was no intensity about this phrase now, and she could talk about her relationship with food in a new way. More important, she was able to understand and forgive herself.

In other sessions, we tapped together on many of the specific incidents that had upset her and made her feel like life was too overwhelming. Among the issues we tapped for were:

- Her feelings about her self-image
- Feeling overwhelmed in her particular classes

- Feeling overwhelmed by her parents' desire that she major in education, when she really wanted to be a physicist

- Her difficulties with relationships with men

- Her difficulties with her roommates (they were much more socially oriented and superficial than she felt herself to be)

- Her very difficult relationships with her mother and father, who were divorced and who each had very different expectations of Nicole and each other.

Whenever I work with a bright, sensitive young person, I find myself wishing that I had had an EFT mentor when I was that age. Thankfully, though, no matter what our age, we can go back and rewrite our history now with EFT. We can tell ourselves a different story about what it all meant.

4

Growing Up Sensitive

What is it like to grow up highly sensitive among people who don't "get" who you are? To facilitate your understanding of the trait of sensitivity and your relationship to it, in this chapter four people I have worked with tell about growing up sensitive and how they reevaluated their childhood experiences.

Gina, John, Madelyn, and Moira (real people, not their real names) grew up in families that didn't notice, honor, or value their sensitivity. It may be more true to say that one or both of each person's parents was highly sensitive but had to shut down their feelings to protect themselves from a lifetime of their own pain and unfulfilled dreams.

Many sensitive children are raised in families that seem practical, industrious, and social, and for whom appearances and "following the rules" are important. A creative, imaginative, quiet child feels very out of place, or even in danger. In some cases, the parents manifest unhealthy, addictive behaviors that create a chaotic scary environment. But if we could look into the parents' deepest hearts for their positive intention behind what looks and feels to their sensitive children like abuse and neglect (and it is), we might find that they were thinking unconsciously that their actions were protecting their children from a similar life of pain. ("Don't get your hopes up, kid—it's a hard world out there. You got to be tough to make it. I'm doing this for your own good.")

Though deep inside, most parents are doing their best to act from love of their children, that is not the message the sensitive children get, just as their parents didn't get that message from the same actions by their own parents. And on and on, back through the generations. In some way that isn't understood, the healing work we do with EFT can heal both the past and the future.

If anything in the following stories touches you, tap up and down the points while you read them. Tap for any memories that come up for you.

Gina: "Tapping Self-Appreciation into Myself"

"People say to me, 'Why do you let things bother you? You get upset so easily!' I had someone tell me that after I decided to leave my job. 'Why not let it roll off your back?' she added. I thought to myself, 'Well, how good are you at that? You think you have no problems. Yet you have allergies, asthma, and other physical conditions. Do you really think there isn't a correlation?'

"I was always sensitive to bright lights, big crowds, and loud music, though I love music. I don't like being around lots of people. I am very hermit-like.

"I know I must have been incredibly sensitive as a child. There were many emotional traumas in my life. I never felt like I had much of a voice. That has caused me problems in my life. I have very decided opinions but had no voice as a child. My father believed that children should be seen and not heard. As a teenager, from fourteen to sixteen, I was really drawn to abstract thought, philosophical things, religion, maybe philosophy more than religion, more than most people I knew in school, but I never had opportunity to express it at home and at school I was so bored.

"I have always been exceptionally sensitive to music. At eleven, I saw *West Side Story*, and I cried because the music was so beautiful. People asked, 'What's the matter?' Singing could bring me to tears.

"I didn't get a chance to sing as a child. My parents were tired of being parents. They didn't encourage the girls to do anything. In grade school, my teacher said I could sing. My parents said, 'Oh yeah, that's nice,' but I was not encouraged to do anything. The irony is that my father was in show business as an acrobatic performer. He loved being in front of crowd, but he never saw that in me.

"I remember my parents had people over one night when I was ten or eleven. They had me come out of my room and sing a song. They said, 'That was wonderful, now go back to your bedroom.' That was the only time they ever encouraged me.

"I really wanted to learn guitar. My mother said, 'Oh, your sister and brother took that, but they didn't like it. I'm sure you won't either.' I convinced her to get me a guitar, and then asked if I could get lessons. I was told, 'You never stick to anything. You have to prove to me that you are not going to waste our money on lessons.' I just took it in that the fault was me. Ten years later, when the guitar was gathering dust, my mother said, 'See, I told you so.' But how did they expect me to maintain interest if they never let me learn? I don't think my mother wanted me to have anything she didn't have.

"As an adult, I stayed in my accounting job way past when I should have left. I should never even have done that work. I was good at it, but I was bored by it, and no one ever encouraged me to think I was worth doing anything else. When I began a couple of years ago to look at why I was in so much pain, I felt anger at myself for not having figured out how to let go of that job. I am sad that I was sad. Now that I have quit, I have to be careful, thinking I have no right to be angry and sad anymore. I feel guilty when I am not happy and blissful that I am no longer in that job. I have to be up, happy, and chipper for my husband.

"It made me angry that I couldn't tough it out. I kept thinking I should be able to do this. Not being able to tough it out would be a failure, a sign of weakness. I should be able to let it roll off me, not let it bother me. That is a philosophy I was raised with. If you got hurt, you would hear, 'Oh it's not that bad, just tough it out.' That carried into emotions, too. I didn't tell my dad I had quit my job because he would see me as a failure. But I knew in my heart that the failure would be there to stay.

"I get frustrated that my body won't do what I want it do to without hurting. I can't push myself like my father can. He can work circles around me. He has a toughness. He just overcomes the body.

"Now I know that the sensitive temperament requires that you pay attention to the body!

"I can stand back and look at my body as a separate entity. I used to find myself talking to it: 'Why can't you work better!' I would work to exhaustion. There is so much to do. I never thought about it until I started doing this EFT healing work, but I realize that those are not healthy beliefs to maintain. With all this pain, my body must be saying, 'You need to give me more rest, not have such high expectations!'

"After I started doing the tapping work, I came to realize I am smarter and more perceptive, more intuitive than I ever knew I was. I know things. I read my husband's mind all the time. I beam stuff out to him.

"When I get rid of anger, I feel more relaxed. I hold anger and tension in my body like a coiled spring. When I tap, I can feel the tenseness draining out of me and I can breathe and relax.

"I think I always knew I was intelligent but I didn't want anyone to know. I wasn't capable of acknowledging that before I did EFT, because I was taught that is being proud and conceited. 'You don't toot your own horn.'

'Don't break your arm patting yourself on the back.' My parents grew up with those impoverished beliefs.

"My grandmother told me she regretted that she did not show more affection and encouragement to her children. She thought they would be spoiled. She saw her son doing the same thing to his kids. She told my dad that she was born out of wedlock. Her mother (this is my great-grandmother) then married a man they found for her who was 'willing to take her as damaged goods.' This husband verbally abused her. So I can see how it gets passed down through the generations.

"The best thing that tapping really does for me is saying, 'I deeply and completely accept myself.' That has had a profound effect on my sense of my own value. I have come to appreciate myself, to recognize myself and my intelligence. Tapping gets this knowing into your belief system. It gets into your cells somehow."

John: "Who Would I Be Without My Melancholy?"

(John was one of the participants in an EFT class I taught. He was on disability and had no job or money. He was bright and a creative writer, unpublished as of yet and also perfectionist (doing one hundred revisions). He said, "I am writing a book. I can't stop and publish it because who will I be when I am no longer writing a book?")

"Being sensitive is a little bit shameful if you are a man. But being sensitive had advantages, so it was also a mixed thing.

"I am sensitive to cold, air conditioning, and overhead lights. As a child, I was extremely sensitive to having my feelings hurt. Even my skin was sensitive. It didn't take much to hurt my feelings. I was angry a lot. My mother and father weren't trying to hurt me. When you are a boy, you attempt to cover up all that emotional stuff, so you keep it to yourself, try not to cry. If you are a boy crying, people make fun of you. There was lots of cruelty by boys (also some from girls), but I perpetuated it, too. It was a combination of mental, psychological, and physical cruelty. I would suddenly change my personality to become someone my sister was really scared of. I was frustrated. I took it out on others, constantly, and vice versa.

"There is this whole thing I concocted to get out of growing up. It has its drawbacks, but it works. I miss being a more powerful person. I would go more places, have more girlfriends, have more things that I wanted. I have traded all that for safety. It's not quite that simple, but sort of. Most of the time I didn't feel that I was making decisions to be this way. Illness came along and knocked me over. There was not a damn thing I could do about it except learn how to rest and go inward.

"I think because I am male that I always kind of pushed aside the notion of being sensitive. It is only recently that I can say I guess it is true. In the early seventies, there was a lot of stuff about sensitive men, that they used their sensitivity to manipulate women. I feared doing that."

The topic of the class John was in was sadness and depression. I opened the class by asking, "What breaks your heart?" That was a prelude to asking, "What in your life, in your past, has broken your heart?" The idea was that all the heartbreaks are those too-painful-to-deal-with feelings and memories that are stored in the body. We discussed this idea, and we talked about what beliefs about ourselves could rise from heartbreak.

Then, in the midst of the EFT work we were doing as a group to clear the trauma of the memories from the body, John said suddenly, "Can I interrupt?" When I told him he could, he offered, "I just realized that I may not want to let go of this melancholy."

John had been coming to the class faithfully and attentively for several weeks, but in each class he said that he wasn't getting any effect from the EFT tapping, or only minimal effect. He wasn't doing it much on his own, but said when he did that it helped "a little."

So we tapped for "not wanting to let go of my melancholy." John began to realize that feeling his melancholy made it possible for him to feel anything at all. Eventually, as we talked about what hidden benefits this melancholy might have for his life, he said with a sheepish smile, "Well, I learned as a child that if you go around like a baby bird with your mouth open, people feed you." And then he said, gulping, "If I let go of my melancholy, I might have to change my identity." The realizations kept coming. "I might have to get a job, I might have to be successful, I might have to express my power, oh shit, I might have to feel how angry I am. If I let go of all this, I won't know who I am."

This shift in his perception of who he is in the world could open the way for more of who he really is to emerge. In this one EFT session, we didn't "solve" all of John's problems. But it was a huge success for him to be able to recognize and admit, to himself and to others, that he had been unconsciously holding himself back with the thought, "If I let go of being sad and feeling/acting like a helpless victim, I might have to change—and I won't know who I am."

I had little contact with John after the class ended, so I don't know how this realization grew in him. He may have decided, consciously or unconsciously, not to change, that it was too hard. But I believe that something inside always changes and opens to new possibilities when we can bring a statement like his to the light of conscious awareness. EFT frequently opens the way for these paradigm-shifting awarenesses. It is our choice whether to utilize them.

Madelyn: Hypervigilant Planning, Trying to Follow the Unwritten Rules

"My sensitivity started as a child with being sensitive emotionally to things, getting my feelings hurt easily. My family called me a crybaby a lot. Your parents always calling you a crybaby is not a good feeling. I got spanked when I was little. At the time, spanking was a common way of raising children. But for me it was way too intense. I was so sensitive that they would only have had to look at me cross-eyed. I wasn't a rebellious kid.

"I don't remember thinking that I got what I deserved. Probably what came out of that for me was a belief that I wasn't safe, never knowing when things would blow up.

"When I look at my father, I think he also had a sensitive temperament. He had a very big startle reflex, a hair-trigger temper. He would startle first, and then be very mad. It was scary for me.

"We moved twice in my high school years, to different cities. As a sensitive person, you need to grow up with a close circle of friends and feel like you have a group. But to go to a whole new group twice stunted me a little. I am not the kind of person who can go up to a table full of kids in the cafeteria and say, 'Hi, I'm new, can I eat with you?'

"As I grew up, being sensitive manifested as being a good friend to people, but liking small groups rather than large groups, because you can make deeper connections in small groups.

"I always thought I was more sensitive to the senses than other people are. When I found out later that I had fibromyalgia, I looked back and could see that I was already more sensitive to pain early in my life. For example, in high school I would have to spend a couple of days in bed with menstrual cramps.

"In my twenties, I continued to escalate with physical symptoms that were suggesting, if I had known enough to see it, that something was way out of balance. I started out with a spastic colon, and then problems with sleep from stress at work, and I got worse. I kept going up the mountain with my symptoms, and then having a plateau, till I hit the next level with breast cancer. That was Pike's Peak.

"I have been exceptionally successful both in school and at work. My sensitivity gives me access to creativity. I have an ability to sense or pick up what it is that people need, and turn that into a creative solution. That is a positive thing. Also, my sensitivity makes me a really good mom. The thing about sensitive people being like the canary the miners used — I know I am picking up stuff before others do. I like to use that at work to help make the place better for everybody.

"I am a planner and a perfectionist. You have to do so much planning to accommodate sensitivity, to make sure you are not in situations that you can't take care of yourself in. Recently, my husband took me to a concert for my birthday. It was so loud that I felt assaulted by the sound waves. It was so hard to see all eight hundred of the other people there having a good time.

"One of the major things is trying to avoid getting my feelings hurt and avoid that whole 'freeze' situation. Over the years, I have learned from those situations too well — I always try to plan my way out of getting into those situations again. The cage gets smaller. And planning never works. I am learning that you can't think yourself out of this.

"When I look back at things that happened to me that had a negative impact, one experience I remember is when I was in sixth grade. We were all lined up to go back inside after playground. There was a girl who had been my best friend, but she was also the queen bee. One day she decided that she didn't like me, and proceeded to tell me in front of other kids how much she hated me. That kind of queen bee person recognizes the sensitive ones and uses them as a target.

"The other imprint was when I was in seventh grade. The eighth graders had a tradition of mentoring seventh graders. I had a party for the seventh graders early in the school year. The next night at the football stadium, a couple of eighth grade girls dressed me up and down in front of everybody for hating the eighth graders. I didn't know that the older grade was supposed to mentor the younger grade; they must not have been doing a very good job of it since I hadn't known. But I was devastated.

"It always seems like there are unwritten rules. Even now, today, I am always trying to see them, plan for them, so I won't trip over them. But that is the whole thing about unwritten rules—you can't see them or plan for them."

Once Madelyn understood that her sensitivity was a trait, and not a fault, she was able to go back into her childhood experiences and reframe them. She learned how to imagine tapping on her child self as she tapped in the present moment on her adult self. She was able to talk to her inner child self frozen in fear and pain, and offer the deeper understanding of her adult self.

As the pain of the early experiences began to dissolve with EFT, Madelyn became a kind of mentor for herself. When she encountered situations in which there seemed to be unwritten rules, she could tap to help herself relax and use her intuition to be aware of all the information in the environment around the situation, as well as remind herself of her exceptional inner strength and intelligence. In this way, she began to develop patience and ease with herself, replacing the constriction of trying too hard that had led to so much physical illness.

Moira: "I Created Clamor So No One Would Notice the Real Me"

"I now understand that I am sensitive and that it is not 'grandstanding.' Growing up, I had a lot of behavior that I now see was my reaction to being so sensitive. I was too stimulated, but that was interpreted as being hard to deal with or being a handful.

"What I see now is that I was being overstimulated pretty much everywhere I went. No one knew that. I didn't know that. All these coping mechanisms came into play. I was trying to get things to be my way. There wasn't a lot of family structure in place. My parents didn't know how to parent. It was chaos. The world always felt chaotic everywhere I went. I desperately wanted to be able to control things. That was sort of a coping mechanism because I couldn't afford to be as vulnerable and receptive as I actually was.

"After I got sick and after an expert on fibromyalgia explained to me about the intuitive-feeling type, things started to make sense to me. I was able to create circumstances that dropped my stimulation level way down to a level where I could feel better, to where I could actually feel how I feel. For most of my life, I had no idea how I was feeling.

"I was like a radar receiver dish moving, scanning, and picking up. I picked up so much from the environment. At first, it was hard to take in the idea I was sensitive. I thought it meant that I was making excuses for myself—lying. Gradually, I thought that if it's true, it would explain a lot. Things started to fall into place. Instead of saying I'm antisocial, I say now that I am an intuitive feeler. Doesn't mean I am a bad person. I can leave and it's OK.

"From my mother's side of the family I got the pressure of 'What did I accomplish today?' On my father's side, it was always 'Prepare for the worst, prepare for the worst, prepare for the worst.' There was no 'Expect the best.' There was no belief in a sustaining safe pattern or meaning behind everything. From my current vantage point, it looks to me that I was an extremely sensitive child and I didn't get the kind of safety, intimacy, and quiet encouragement I needed, so I tried to soldier on. I was always trying to be a good girl. Life felt like meaningless chaos without spirit to it.

"I came away from my family with the idea that 'I am a bossy unpleasant person, smart, talented, but not lovable.' I lived my life at a very high volume; I turned the volume up on my own conduct because I felt so drowned out by my surroundings.

"I don't remember my childhood. I can't point to one thing. I was not raped, didn't go to war. I just look back and say, "Oh my gosh, the whole thing."

"I didn't feel safe inside myself and wasn't really present in myself. I lost the ability to know that I was 'home.' I didn't know how I felt at any time of the day or night. When I was with another person, I experienced that as a traumatic event. There was hitting in my family when I was a little kid. I realize that other people seemed dangerous to me. I did my best to give a facsimile of what I would be if I could actually be present.

"I am actually over here to the side of my body. I didn't want anyone to see me; that was too dangerous. So I created a lot of clamor, extroverted activity, so no one would see me. I seem very extroverted. I also drank socially. Drinking would take the cork out of my inhibitions. I would be a very amusing, great storyteller. Creating a whirlwind of activity, a lot of noise, and interesting things to look at or hear so no one would ever notice the real me over there—a diversionary camouflage.

"It is not that it was inauthentic. It is what I would do if I could really be alive. Life comes down to knowing: Do I like this or not? When you are outside your body, you don't know. There is this terrible starvation going on. I am terrified of intimacy; I feel like I'm not there. I lost the ability to be alone with myself, or to be myself, or to be with myself or with anyone else.

"Unbeknownst to me, I was deeply unhappy, but I thought that was just the deal. I think that my mother might also be deeply unhappy and thinks that's just the deal. It isn't necessary to be that unhappy. We couldn't have understood that. I think she thinks that a life is basically unhappy, but you just do it anyway. There is the soldiering on. My dad just didn't go to the emotions. Neither Mom nor Dad was available to me emotionally.

"Being around people, I can't stay inside myself and stay in touch. I am not ready yet to be around people. It is exhausting. I want to stay in touch with my own feelings.

"When I think of my past, I feel grief and terrible despair, loss, and hopelessness. I can hardly bear to look at it. Exactly like PTSD [posttraumatic stress disorder]. If I start thinking about it, then I start reliving it. There is no way out. If I try to talk with my mom about how I feel, I get waves of pity from her. That is terrifying. It confirms my feeling that my situation is hopeless. You don't know there is another way; stuff you absorbed as a child, you think that is just the way life is.

"The feeling I got from my mom is that I am a baby from a litter who is deformed and not going to be OK; it is hopeless and so sad. This life that had so much promise is a mangled hopeless sad thing. It makes me feel sick. In her life, I was the runt of the litter; no one loved me.

"EFT gave me a practical framework to act in partnership as a friend to my mysterious body and to call on the mysterious powers of my body to support me in that new paradigm.

"Now, if I am alone long enough to settle in, I am getting to the point where I can tell how I feel. I need a lot of solitude to settle into my body, to feel alive. I can stay with myself and tell how I'm feeling. I walk my dog at night near the lake and it is so beautiful. Once the people are all gone, the atmosphere changes. Everything is very still and very present. I would cry. I would walk and cry every night. Gradually, I began to feel joy. Peace.

"Now I am noticing when something feels a certain kind of beautiful, true, authentic, spiritual, touchstone inside. Positive."

All four of these people talk of the dysfunction of their families. I would guess that in each set of their parents at least one was highly sensitive. But this parent would likely have been raised by at least one parent who had so covered over and denied, or been overwhelmed by, their own sensitivity that the child growing up would have had no model for how to respond to the world.

Many of the characteristics of the sensitive temperament are reflected in their stories. They all tried to be what they thought they "should be," each of them developed an alternative way of being in the world to survive, each of them became ill, each of them had important realizations about the connection between their sensitive temperaments and their wellness, each of them came to value their sensitivity in a profound way.

Gina, John, Madelyn, and Moira also each used EFT over a period of several months to years, and experienced differing degrees of healing and transformation. EFT isn't like a pill that you take until you are "well," and then you throw away the bottle and the prescription. I think EFT is a lifestyle, especially for a highly sensitive person.

We are probably always going to feel the intensity of physical, emotional, and spiritual experience more keenly than most people. But we don't have to be at the effect of it. We can use our sensitivity in positive, powerful, life-changing, and world-changing ways.

It is a blessing to have this tool of EFT literally at our fingertips, offering an ever-ready opportunity for healing and adding the possibility of deeper meaning to misfortune. But it is up to us to use it and, as John discovered, the price of healing may be deep change. Not everyone is ready to be all they can be. We haven't had many models for how to do this. We are learning together.

5

How Can EFT Help
with Sensitivity?

Being highly sensitive has its blessings and its drawbacks, sometimes both, often simultaneously. Much of my work has been to share how to use EFT to heal the wounds of the sensitive nature, so that we are empowered to use our gifts in the service of ourselves, our families, our communities, and the world.

There is no best way to apply EFT to the problems that arise from being so sensitive to the overwhelm of daily living, to say nothing of trauma. Over the years, I have developed three approaches that work well: List Problem Phrases, Break Out of the Cage of the PASST (Pain, Anger, Sadness, Stress, Trauma), and Story Map.

List Problem Phrases

In a stream-of-consciousness style, write down anything you can think of about having a highly sensitive temperament that you feel has been a problem for you.

Pull out specific phrases, thoughts, images, and feelings and make a list. From these thoughts and images, create brief "problem phrases" that you can use as the tapping Setup and for tapping on the points. Or you can go back to chapter 1 and pick out phrases that you responded to. The idea is to come up with a list of phrases and images that trigger a feeling in you.

At each tapping session, pick one or more phrases from your list to begin with as the EFT Setup, and start tapping on the Karate Chop point. Here are some examples of HST problem phrases (underlined) you can use in the Setup:

> *Even though <u>I worry that I am too sensitive</u>, I deeply and completely love and accept myself anyway*

> *Even though <u>I feel too deeply</u>, I love and accept myself anyway.*

> *Even though <u>I am so open to others' emotions</u>, I completely love and respect myself anyway.*

Then use the problem phrases to tap on the tapping points. Be open to thoughts and memories as you do this. As they occur to you, add them to the problem phrases while tapping on the points.

Here are some more problem phrase possibilities for HST:

Even though:

> *I am easily hurt and upset...*
> *I don't like conflict...*
> *It's hard to stop feeling sad sometimes...*

I can't watch the news or sad or violent movies...

I get depressed easily...

I get overwhelmed...

I can't stand large crowds...

I can't take loud noise...

I don't like hectic environments...

I wish I were tougher and could let things roll off me more easily...

I think my sensitivity is a weakness...

I think something is wrong with me, that it is my fault...

I wish things didn't bother me so much...

I wish my emotions weren't so obvious to other people...

I wish I could let things go and not worry so much...

I hide my sensitivity from others...

I like to add comforting and encouraging phrases to the standard EFT Setup statement ending, such as:

I deeply and completely love and accept myself anyway, and I honor myself for how hard it is.

When you are first learning EFT, it is a good idea to follow the Basic Recipe, as detailed in chapter 2. So take each Setup phrase, tap on the Karate Chop point while you say that phrase three times, and then tap through the points with the problem phrase. Repeat this process until you feel a shift, or a new thought comes to you.

Break Out of the Cage of the PASST (Pain, Anger, Sadness, Stress, Trauma)

Begin by asking yourself:

1. What have people said to me about my sensitivity?

   Tap on:

   Even though people [my mother, father, friend, boss] have always said _____, I deeply and completely love and accept myself anyway.

2. How has that made me feel? Where do I feel these feelings in my body?

   Tap on:

   Even though what they said makes me feel so sad and angry, I accept that I have those feelings, and I want to find a different way to think about this.

3. What did I come to believe about myself as a result?

   Tap on:

   Even though I thought there must be something wrong with me, and I thought that I wasn't enough somehow, I love and accept myself.

4. Choose a specific disturbing incident from your life connected with being sensitive. Make a movie or inner story of the specific incident. Give it a title. Note details: clear, fuzzy, movement, still, sound, silent, and so on.

   Tap on the title:

   Even though I have this _____ [title] story in my body about being sensitive, I deeply and completely love and accept myself.

Tap while you watch and feel the story or movie unfold.

Tap on the worst parts.

Tap on all the aspects.

Note what has changed in your response to the story after you tap. Check your level of intensity on the 0-to-10 scale.

Story Map

In a Story Map, you outline the main ideas in the story of a representative event in your life. The Story Map easily translates into phrases useful in your EFT sessions. For practitioners, having the client do a Story Map reduces the time spent gathering information, so session time can be devoted to the actual tapping work.

The Story Map is an especially useful tool in a class setting. In this case, each participant fills out the Story Map beforehand with his or her own issue. Then everyone can tap along when a volunteer steps forward for a session in class. The other participants keep their own issue in the back of their mind as they tap along, thus borrowing the benefits of the volunteer's session. Much healing change can happen in a Borrowing Benefits session.

These are the Story Map statements to complete:

"I had to _____ or else_____."

A belief [behavior, outlook on life, self-image] about this that I got from my family is _____.

That created a problem in my life because [or when] _____.

*A good example of that is that time when _____
[particular, specific].*

*The worst part of that particular incident was
_____.*

That made me feel _____.

It made me think I was _____.

I feel that in my body here: _____ [name part].

*Sometimes I even think maybe I don't deserve
_____.*

But deep inside, I yearn for _____.

If I had that, I would feel _____.

*So now I forgive myself. I was doing the best I could.
I choose to _____ instead.*

This Story Map is simple, though not always easy to
fill out. Just coming up with the answers may be a triggering experience. In the process of tapping, you might take
each of the completed sentences, make a Setup statement
from it, and tap through the story this way, until no part
of the story is still a trigger. It is also possible to use these
sentences more fluidly in the EFT session, adding them as
phrases in the tapping process as the need arises.

The following client experience will show you how
the Story Map process works.

Ann: "Setting My Wild Pony Energy Free"

This is Ann's Story Map:

I had to *hide my true self* or else *I would get in trouble or
be attacked by mental cruelty.*

A belief about this that I got from my family is *the whole family must conform and agree with Mom.*

That created a problem in my life because *I followed her desires, not mine. There is still shame in me for not working and having a career, shame for having health challenges. And I have fatigue and food allergies that get in the way of my cooking and living the life I want.*

A good example of that is that at *every dinnertime I was bracing myself for the energy that was coming at me.*

The worst part of that was *when she attacked me she felt like an energy vampire, and I felt responsible to keep her in a good mood. I thought if I stood up to her she would die.*

That made me feel *that my own feelings were not allowed. I feel helpless, silenced, stuck, and invisible. I feel angry, ashamed, and afraid.*

It made me think *I was not important, that she didn't care what I thought, and that I will always be pounced on and judged.*

I feel that in my body here: *I feel dissociated and spaced out. My throat is tight, I can't sit up straight; I am hunched over. I can't find my voice to express what I feel and think.*

Sometimes I even think maybe I don't deserve *to be here.*

But deep inside, I yearn *to feel accepted.*

If I had that I would feel *confident, loved, like I belong.*

So now I forgive myself. I was doing the best I could. I choose to *learn how to love and accept myself instead.*

This is Ann's back-story behind the Story Map:

"I felt a strange cruel energy in my family dynamic, and my strategy was to space out and not feel it. It resulted in feeling that I have to be quiet and hide my true self, or I will get in trouble or be attacked by mental cruelty.

"My mother is a narcissist; it's all her and no me, so to speak. The message I got is that we (the whole family) must conform and agree with Mom. Although I don't have one incident, there were what I call 'sarcasm dinners.' When I was in school, we all ate dinner together and mom reigned like a queen with her 'humor,' which was sarcasm and mental cruelty (ha, ha). For years, I thought I was boring and not funny enough because I thought humor was sarcasm and I could never do it.

"Mom was a 'feminist' who joked about running away from the family. Us kids got in the way of her brilliant career. She put down everything and everyone not like her: traditional women, child care, lawyers, farmers, republicans, her students, her chairman, men, rich people, anyone! And we all got to hear it at dinner. She was a history professor. Intellect was king. Feelings were a strange undercurrent of resentment.

"Today I have food allergies and I think it is related! At the time, I thought Mom was 'funny,' but I wanted to eat fast and leave the table. There was no nourishment there; the food was toxic. Then later I realized that many of the people she put down were like me: sensitives. She hates gardeners and farmers (I grow organics in the country) and women who don't work in a high-powered career or don't have lots of education (I was forced to go to the college that she chose). She hates cooking (I am a whole-foods cook).

"She doesn't attack me directly, just all my values. She continually questions and doubts all my life choices. She wants me to be an extroverted career woman, like her. She is upset that I don't have her values and lifestyle and wants me to change. There is a constant subtle undercurrent of hate and resentment. Dad backs her up but is generally quieter; I think he may also be sensitive. I often think it's her sharp, left-brain intellect with clever words versus my subtle feelings world. I don't have words to fight back. So I just take it and feel bad energy. She feels like an energy vampire. When I was in high school, she would get mad at Dad and tell me all about it, like I was her therapist! Lots of resentment dumped on me.

"I got educated and tried the career route, but it's not me, at least not like that. I would rather cook, make art, or write about healing. I tried to force myself to be intellectual, a career woman, and outgoing, but I got chronic fatigue and had to stop. Then I realized I had followed her desires, not mine. There is still shame in me for not working and having a career, shame for having health challenges. In her and Dad's mind, career work and higher education are God!

"Since Mom is a narcissist, she never asked or cared what I was interested in. I just did whatever she wanted to avoid being 'sarcasmed.' I was made to take piano, but I wanted to learn how to do batik. I was told not to ask spiritual questions, so I quit asking. I was interested in art, but so what? No space for me. I am afraid to show my true self (a cook, a sensitive, gardener, spiritual person, home designer, etc). And I have fatigue and food allergies that get in the way of my cooking and living the life I want.

"I have a very different lifestyle than most of my family and I am afraid to show it because there will be mental cruelty and attacks and I'll have to justify my path. I am too scared to speak. I like ideas and have an interest in natural healing, cooking, and spirituality but can't find my voice to express them. I write about them but can't imagine getting them out into the world, which I imagine is full of intellectuals ready to pounce on me and judge me! Or abandon or ignore me.

"I notice when I get triggered, I don't have words. I think I polarize to my right brain. No words. I notice that when I tap on my own, I just think the words and don't say them out loud. I wonder if the spaced-out strategy comes from an inner infant, preverbal place.

"I feel helpless, quiet, stuck, and invisible. I want to feel accepted, confident, and loved."

Ann's issue was global (the family patterns), but we needed to begin working with something specific.

Tapping for the "Sarcasm Dinners"

We chose her family dinner experiences, the "sarcasm dinners," and when she couldn't think of one specific one, I asked her to create a movie in her mind of a typical example. We used the title "Sarcasm Dinner." She chose a descriptive phrase: "I had to de-Self for my mother's protection."

I knew that we probably wouldn't be able to solve these issues for Ann in one session, but I wanted to help her open a space inside herself for a different way of experiencing herself, which would plant a seed that would generate change over time. In doing EFT, I am not always looking for the "one-minute fix-it wonder." Instead, I am helping the person to establish a generative, evolving force inside herself that, if she nourishes it, will grow and invite deeper change from within.

The primary emotions Ann felt when she thought of the Sarcasm Dinner was anger, shame, and fear. The intensity for these feelings was off the 10-point scale, at 12 or 13.

We tapped first for the movie title "Sarcasm Dinner," bringing in the feelings of anger and fear and all these body responses, until she could see the scene and stay relaxed.

I chose some of the charged phrases from the Story Map and from what she wrote to use as Setup statements, and worked with them with EFT one by one:

Even though…

> *my mother is a narcissist — it is all her, not me…*
>
> *she questions and doubts my life choices…*
>
> *she feels like an energy vampire…*
>
> *I am afraid to show my true self…*
>
> *food became toxic to me…*
>
> *I followed her desires, not mine…*

I can't find my voice to express what I feel and think…
I imagine I will always be pounced on and judged…
I will be ignored or abandoned…
I feel helpless, silenced, stuck, and invisible…
I deeply and completely love and accept myself.

We also talked about and did some tapping rounds for the feeling of dissociation and the "inner infant, pre-verbal place" that got triggered when she was in situations that reminded her of being with her mother. This was a thought that came up as we were tapping that hadn't occurred to her before.

Awakening the Wild Pony Within

As so often happens in an EFT session when we have softened the hard, constricted place inside in the heart and the gut and the breathing, where all the repressed feelings have been held, Ann began to be aware of another energy inside her. She described it as a "wild pony energy that wants to do something outrageous!"

I love it when a strong new inner current emerges. It is an opportunity for me to use my intuition and my creativity, and to invite the same from the person with whom I am working. I am always thinking what words and phrases can best describe in this situation the positive aspects of a powerful alternative to feeling helplessly victimized.

We developed the image and the feeling in her body of this wild pony, running free and strong across wide-open space, feeling the wind in her mane and the sun on her back, full of endless energy, exhilarating in choosing her own path, confident in her stride, feeling a part of her community. I chose phrases suggested by the image of the pony that resonated with an alternative to the words she used about herself. I just let my own imagination run free as we tapped. A Native American figure entered her image, as a friend, guide, and companion to the wild pony. We integrated all the images and feelings as well as the Native American figure into the tapping phrases.

By the end of the session, Ann felt energized, relaxed, and optimistic. She was standing up straight and her throat felt open. She felt safe to explore using her own voice. In fact, she was realizing that, in spite of what her mother said and thought, she had created her life in the way she wanted it. She felt brimming with wild pony energy.

After the session, I encouraged her to work with the symbol of a wild pony in her life: draw it, sculpt it, look for a figure or a totem of a wild pony, find a picture, write about it, meditate on it, tap on it often. I believe that when we honor these images that come to us, when we are asleep or awake, we honor the energy that they represent in us and invite it to grow. Our healing lies in taking actions like this.

Later Ann wrote to me:

> Since my session with you, I have been seeing many horses, on TV, towed in trailers (this is Texas), in picture books.

I now have conversations with my wild pony! She wants me to take art lessons and learn about local herbs. I see her running through a field of goldenrod. And I am the Native American riding and talking with her. Isn't imagination fun? I have been drawing ponies, too, and tapping regularly.

I am enjoying hearing how EFT works with intuition. It gives me hope that there is a way to use sensitivity instead of thinking it is a burden. It can be useful and helpful. That is new for me and I love to see it demonstrated. And I am inspired that a person who is sensitive like you can travel to England and present in front of people!

I thought all sensitives were cowering in a corner somewhere…I want a new vision.

There was a lot more that EFT could do with Ann's story and her issues, but her comments let me know that healing was awakened in her. We could say "unbridled"!

The three strategies I've given you here for working with the highly sensitive temperament have been useful to me in nearly every session with a client or in a class, and personally in my own tapping. Sometimes I mix them together or flow from one to another in a given session. I have made working with the life challenges of HST one of my specialties, partly because I am one, too, so I understand the temperament.

Set Your Own Wild Pony Energy Free

1. Write a paragraph, a page, or more about your experience of having a highly sensitive temperament. Include feelings, images, memories, beliefs, and expectations—whatever comes up. Don't censor yourself; let it flow. This is for your eyes only. Tap for whatever you feel yourself reacting to, until you can read with acceptance what you wrote.

2. Answer and respond to the questions posed in "Break Out of the Cage of the PASST." Tap for whatever triggers an emotional response.

3. Complete the sentences in the Story Map, and use each statement as a jumping-off place for an EFT session. Let yourself be flexible, creative, and self-encouraging with this.

Highly sensitive people, like Ann, are often artistic, athletic, or both. They are consciously (or unconsciously) spiritually oriented, intuitive, and empathic, and are likely in healing or service-oriented work and activities. They may not be aware of their sensitivity. Like Ann, they may have been dismissed, shamed, or unacknowledged so often that they have developed a hard shell or a sad depression, and they may no longer even notice how sensitive they are. But they all have a wild pony within them, waiting to run free!

The next chapter will help you to reframe the feelings and the limiting beliefs that you have developed over time as a result of feeling so different from other people. You will learn how to transform them into feelings and beliefs that celebrate who you are.

6

Turn Problems
into Preferences

In our diligent search as sensitive people and perfectionists to find all the things wrong with us and correct them, it doesn't occur to most of us that we are misusing our energy. Many of us use our energy to develop red herrings like illness, chronic fatigue, or addictions to distract ourselves and others from noticing that we are really just "selfishly" doing what we want to do (instead of what we "should" be doing).

Instead of framing our sensitivity as a fault, a not-enough-ness, and pushing it away, let's welcome it and celebrate it, and use EFT to enlarge and deepen its gifts.

Make a list of what you like least about being sensitive, such as:

- I am not good at small talk.

- I feel what everyone else is feeling.

- Being so sensitive makes me fearful.

- I don't have good boundaries.

- I seem to become the other person.
- I lose myself.
- I try to protect everyone.
- I put other people's needs before mine.

Add what you like best about being sensitive to the Setup phrase:

I deeply and completely love and accept myself, and:

…being so empathic makes me very understanding.

…I am able to see/sense to the heart of a matter.

…I am deeply attuned to beauty.

…I have a deep connection with spirit.

Tapping to Enhance, Expand, Enlarge, and Deepen Your Gifts

Let's start with that tapping list of the problems we experience from our sensitivity and reframe them as our gifts. Then we can make them even better.

The following words are mine, just to give you an example. Change them to fit you or find better ones. Maybe you like to speak in superlatives. Maybe you have more profound or more spiritual ways of expressing what is truly the best, loveliest, and greatest about you—go for it. Use your best words, ones that make you light up inside.

Even though…

~~I worry that I am too sensitive.~~

I love that I am so sensitive, and I choose to deepen and expand it in powerful and appropriate ways.

~~I feel so deeply.~~

I have this wonderful capacity to feel deeply. I choose to accept it as an honor, and learn how to share what I know in ways that are helpful.

~~I am so open to others' emotions.~~

I have the gift of being able to know people deeply, even to know who they are behind the masks they use to protect themselves. I choose to connect with what is best in them, and stay steady with that, so they can come to see the beauty in themselves as well. I choose to protect myself from their negativity. It just bounces off and away from me.

~~I am easily hurt and upset.~~

I am exquisitely sensitive to my own tender feelings, and I acknowledge and honor my feelings for letting me know when I am leaving my center. I choose to be surprised to remember more and more times when I was able to hear something upsetting and maintain a sense of my own truth.

~~I don't like conflict.~~

I have a deep appreciation for harmony and unity, and I choose to be even more surprised and delighted to discover how many times a day I can feel it. I know the more I am aware of my own deep harmony, the more harmony there is in the world.

~~It's is hard to stop feeling sad sometimes.~~

I know I have the ability to hold on to a feeling by talking to myself about the situation, so I choose to discover how many things I can find to say about myself that are positive and that make me happy.

~~I can't watch the news or sad or violent movies.~~

I am very responsive to the stories I hear and see in the media, and I choose what to pay attention to so I can fill my world with joy, fun, and comfort for me. I choose to be fascinated to watch humanity learning and growing, even (or especially) from its mistakes. I trust the flow of the universe, and trust that my awareness of humanity's goodness can flow through even the "bad news."

~~I get depressed easily.~~

I feel so deeply about my life and the world. I choose to use my strengths and creativity to make a difference right where I am, right now.

~~I get overwhelmed.~~

~~I can't stand large crowds.~~

~~I can't take loud noise.~~

~~I don't like hectic environments.~~

~~I wish I were tougher and could let things roll off of me more easily.~~

I do my best to take good care of myself. I choose to find even better and more effective ways to let myself know that I am the best and most valuable me there is!

~~I think my sensitivity is a weakness~~.

I like that I am sensitive. I choose to love, appreciate, and honor this powerful, world-changing soul quality that I have been so blessed with. The world needs what I have to offer! I am ready to be more!

~~I think something is wrong with me, that it is my fault~~.

I think that I am a good person. I choose to open to what I know in my deepest heart that I can become! I love and appreciate and honor this precious being that I am!

~~I wish things didn't bother me so much~~.

I am glad that I am so aware. I choose to trust the Universe to handle the problems, and I use my awareness and my energy to make a difference in this world that I care so much about.

~~I wish my emotions weren't so obvious to other people~~.

~~I hide my sensitivity from others~~.

People always know what I am feeling. I choose to honor and celebrate who I am, and appreciate that people always know where I stand. I choose to stand up and be known for my best and most outstanding ideas.

Now Celebrate!

Tap using the normal EFT spots. But instead of saying "Even though…" try saying "Especially because…"

Especially because I love that I am so sensitive, I choose to deepen and expand my sensitivity in powerful wonderful ways.

Especially because I have this fabulous capacity to feel deeply, I choose to accept it as an honor, and learn how to share what I know in ways that are helpful.

Especially because I like that I am sensitive, I choose to love, appreciate, and honor this powerful, world-changing soul quality that I have been so blessed with. The world needs what I have to offer! I am ready to be more!

Especially because I believe that I am a good person, I choose to open to what I know in my deepest heart that I can become! I love, appreciate, and honor this precious being that I am!

I choose to trust the Universe to handle the problems, and I use my awareness and my energy to make a difference in this world that I care so much about.

Continue tapping beginning with the phrase "Especially because" (EB):

EB I have this wonderful gift of being able to think and speak in abstract big-picture, profound concepts, I choose to deepen and strengthen my ability to be an "imagineer," and I use my manifestation ability even better so that the goodness I sense has a space to live in, in this world.

EB being cooperative and diplomatic is important to me, I choose to break the rules that aren't working for me and make new ones that feel right, in ways that still honor other people's integrity and intentions.

EB I hunger for deep and meaningful relationships, I make creating and maintaining a good and satisfying relationship with myself my first priority. I value personal growth, authenticity, and integrity. I choose to discover my own strengths and excellence, and do everything I can to enlarge them.

EB I am internally deeply caring, I choose to take just as good care of myself as I do of _____.

EB I am deeply committed to the positive and the good, I choose to honor that commitment to myself!

EB I have a strong personal morality, I choose to stand even taller in my own strong life!

EB I often make extraordinary sacrifices for someone/something I believe in, I choose myself!

EB I have a good imagination, I choose to find amazing ways of bringing magic into my life where there was only misery before. Evolution itself depends on how good I get at this!

EB I think I am unusual and unique, I choose to stand up for myself and express who I am with love and a light heart. No one can resist that.

EB I have a mission to bring peace to the world, I choose a mission of bringing peace into my own life.

EB I am sensitive, I understand now that the world needs to know more about this!

EB I am sensitive, I can discover many powerful world-changing figures in history. I can model people *like Homer, the Virgin Mary, Hans Christian Andersen, Princess Diana, Gandhi, Shakespeare. They were sensitive idealists just like me. They would understand me.*

(Notice that you don't have to apply these phases only to the issues of sensitivity!)

I would guess that many, perhaps most, of the people in history who have made an impact on our inner lives, our art, our philosophy, our healing modalities, and even our legal and political systems had highly sensitive temperaments. They were successful because of their sensitivity. This continues to be true. Possibly, the reverse is true, too—many people who are not able to manage the intensity of living in the world with a highly sensitive temperament give up, are beaten down once too often, or take refuge in an altered state of consciousness. There is a great waste of human potential there.

With EFT in our toolboxes, however, we have the opportunity to befriend ourselves in the deepest way and prevent this waste. Imagine this: each time we clear some old hurt or toxic feeling out of our energy field, or help someone else to do that, we are making the world a better place. In the next chapter, you will learn how to heal your own broken heart.

7

What Broke Your Heart?

Let's go deeper now into how we might tap for the emotional issues that can arise in the life of a sensitive person.

Most of us don't have any problem coming up with painful memories. We may be less familiar with this challenge: being in the throes of one of our most effective limiting behaviors or suffering from a physical pain and, at the same time, having the presence of mind to ask ourselves what might be the origin, deep in the past, of our feeling this way today. If you are feeling overwhelmed by what is going on in your life and how you feel about it, you might not even be able to think of where to start with EFT.

Tapping to Heal Your Broken Heart

To feel into what might be going on inside so that you can begin to approach your own healing from the inside out with EFT, try asking yourself some evocative questions: What broke my heart? When did something die in me, or get blocked or shut down?

Here are some other questions that can help you get to the key experiences in your life that are asking for healing:

- What does this remind me of?
- If I could live life over again, what person or event would I prefer to skip?
- When was the last time I cried, and why?
- Who/what makes me angry, and why?
- What is my biggest sadness or regret?
- What is missing to make my life perfect?
- What are three fears I would rather not have?
- What do I wish I had never done?

Write out or tape yourself talking about your experiences. Then take each of the sentences of your story or journal entry that carry a charge for you, and turn it into a tapping sequence.

Go deeper. Ask yourself: What did I lose as a result? A painful experience makes us feel that we have lost our sense of connection, belonging, safety, peace, joy, integrity, or wholeness. Honor yourself for how hard this has been and tap for this deep loss.

For a sensitive person, painful experiences go deeper and hurt more. Here are some more tools that will be helpful as you make your way into your own healing with EFT. This insightful excerpt from *Tapping Your Amazing Potential with EFT,* by Betty Moore-Hafter, an

EFT practitioner and certified clinical hypnotherapist, will help you to tap your way through some of what comes up as you process those painful experiences in your past, or the present. Though it is written to EFT practitioners, you can use the process on yourself. At the end of the excerpt is a list that can help you to be creative with the second half of your Setup phrase. It offers some wonderfully affirming phrases to add to or replace the Setup phrase "I deeply and completely love and accept myself." In my own work, I use this page from Betty's book all the time.

Complex Tapping with Affirming Phrases and "Flow"
by Betty Moore-Hafter

This section offers ideas for going deeper into issues and for using the EFT process in a flexible manner. Reframing and other affirming phrases can be included, and sometimes we may use a narrative flow of words as we tap.

1. Going deeper

When we tap with people, we become very intuitive. They also become more intuitive about their own issues. The moments after a round of EFT, as we both sit quietly experiencing the effects of the tapping, perhaps with eyes closed, either of us may receive intuitive hunches about where to go next. If you get a feeling that there are deeper issues and more complexity under the surface, then it's good to ask some questions, such as:

As you sit quietly for a moment after that round of tapping, just notice any thoughts or feelings that come into your awareness. What are you experiencing?

Did that round of tapping stir up anything? Just notice what comes into your mind.

Does this situation [this feeling, this problem] remind you of anything?

"What does this remind you of?" is one of Gary Craig's favorite questions to get to core issues, and it is often amazing what comes up. You know you're on to something when people say, "Well, I don't know why this comes to mind, but it does remind me of [so-and-so]…I hadn't thought of that in years."

It is remarkable what each of us knows on an intuitive level; we just don't realize that we know it. Simple questions about the source of an issue can often take things deeper. And when we answer "off the top of our head" or "just guess" or say "the first thing that comes to mind," the conscious mind is less likely to get in the way.

What might be the possible cause of this feeling or belief? If you knew the source of it from your past, what might it be?

What's your theory about where this comes from? What's your best guess?

If you did know, what would it be? (Just off the top of your head.)

It is fascinating that our bodies often hold emotion and conflict in ways so familiar to us that our language says it all: "That person is a pain in the neck." "This problem is a headache." "I'm sick to my stomach over this." Louise Hay's *You Can Heal Your Life* is a good resource for thinking metaphorically, with lists of physical ailments and associated emotional issues.

When you suspect deeper issues or you are making little progress tapping for a physical issue, ask a few metaphorical questions [you can do this for yourself, or a practitioner can do it for a client]. Usually, there is an instant recognition—"Oh my gosh, that's it!"—or else the question is simply not on track and we let it go.

> *Since we're working on back pain, I'm just wondering: Is there any burden you're carrying? Or is there anyone or anything you can't get off your back?*
>
> *Even though I have to take care of my elderly mother and no one helps me, it's too much to carry.*
>
> *Even though I can't get my brother off my back...*
>
> *You said these jaw problems started after your divorce. Sometimes people hold anger and resentment in the jaw area. Do you think there might be any connection? Even though I still resent the divorce and I'm holding that resentment in my jaw...*

We can also ask open-ended questions:

> *If you knew what emotion your body is holding in your _____, what might it be?* (Whatever first comes to mind, just say it out loud.)

A word of caution: We are most respectful when we keep in mind that each of us is the expert on ourselves alone; none of us is the expert on another person. If you are a practitioner and the questions that attempt to probe deeper don't ring bells for your client, even if you suspect they're on target, it is best to let them go, and let go of any judgment as well. We may be planting seeds of awareness that will help people go further when the time is right.

2. Breaking down the complex issue into tappable parts

One of the key principles that Gary Craig teaches is the importance of being specific. If we tap for broad, global issues, there is less immediate progress. Specific events are easier to work with. In addition, any emotional freedom that is accomplished generalizes into the whole complex issue, and the entire thing usually becomes lighter and less upsetting. Good questions to ask are:

Can you give an example of this problem in action?

Tell about a specific incident that illustrates the problem.

What is one of the worst times you felt this way? Describe the specific event. What happened?

3. Working with a specific event

Gary Craig's Watch the Movie Technique is an excellent way to proceed. The client makes a brief mental movie of the event and gives it a title. Then as she or he tells the story, you stop and tap whenever there is any emotional intensity, until the client can relate the whole movie with a neutral feeling.

If this were a movie, how long would it be? (We need it to be short, three to five minutes. If it's too long, break it into smaller segments or just choose the highlights.)

If it were a movie, what would be the title?

When you say the title, do you feel intense? (If so, tap for, "Even though I feel this intensity about "_____" [the title]...)

Now run the movie in your mind, or narrate it out loud, tell me what's happening, and whenever you feel anything at all, tell me and we'll tap for it.

Now run through the first part again: Do you feel any more intensity?

For a holistic approach, it can also be useful to gather more information before tapping, or at any point in the process. Here are some specific questions to gather information from the different levels of a holistic approach (physical, mental, emotional, spiritual) and different sensory channels of perception (visual, auditory, kinesthetic). Each of these may reveal tappable aspects of the event.

What do you see when you think about what happened?

What do you hear when you think about the incident?

What do you tell yourself about it?

How does it make you feel? What emotions do you experience?

Where in your body do you feel it? What are the physical sensations?

What judgments do you hold about yourself?

How does this diminish your spirit and keep you from feeling good about yourself?

One question that invariably tunes in to the emotional pain is:

What upsets you the most about this?

4. Adding affirming phrases

It is important not to hurry the process, and it may be necessary to do quite a bit of tapping for the negative emotions before there is enough space inside to bring in positive, affirming messages. Then it can feel reassuring to state an intention for healing, a willingness for something to change, and further self-acceptance and self-affirmation:

Even though…. I'm willing to see this differently.

Even though…. I want to bring some healing to this situation.

Even though… I honor myself for how hard that was. I did the best I could.

More specific affirmations can be formulated as the tapping continues, by you and by your client as you work together.

5. Narrative Flow

With so much to tap for, it is sometimes useful to use a narrative flow of words while tapping. Pull this together from the notes you've taken, using your client's own words. In practice, it might sound something like the following example.

An Example of Complex Tapping: "The Night From Hell"

This participant in an EFT workshop is a young mother. The event is that she let her baby cry at night, following the advice of a book instead of trusting her intuition and her feelings.

Tapping on the Karate Chop point, she stated the "Even though" three times:

Even though I went through that "Night from Hell," I deeply and completely accept myself.

Even though I let my baby cry, I'm still a good person.

Even though I still feel terribly guilty, I love and accept myself (adding the affirming phrase) and I want to forgive myself. I was doing the best I could.

She tapped the points:

Eyebrow: *It was a Night from Hell.*

Side of Eye: *I let my baby cry.*

Under Eye: *I feel so guilty about it.*

Under Nose: *What a Night from Hell!*

Chin: *I let her cry and cry.*

Collarbone: *I feel so guilty about that.*

Under Arm: *Night from Hell—she cried and cried.*

Top of Head: *I feel so guilty.*

Then she switched to affirming phrases:

Karate Chop again: *Even so, I'm still a good person.*

Inside Wrist: *I was doing the best I could.*

Top of Hand: *I choose to forgive myself. I was doing the best I could.*

Deep breath, eyes closed. What are you experiencing?

"I'm mainly mad at myself for listening to the book and not trusting my own instincts."

We proceed, continuing to refer to her description of the event on the questionnaire.

She does a second round of tapping:

Karate Chop point:

Even though I'm mad at myself for not trusting my own instincts, I want to accept myself and forgive myself.

And even though I still see her little face, her tears, so sad, and I hear her screams, and I feel like I really let her down —I hate myself for that —I want to accept myself and forgive myself. I was doing the best I could.

And even though I'm mad at the book, too —what an awful way to treat a baby! —I forgive myself for listening to the book. I was really trying to be a good mother.

Adding affirming phrases:

...and I'm willing to consider that this is how we learn. I learned that doesn't work for me. I'm willing to know and believe that no lasting harm was done. I'm willing to consider that my baby has forgotten all about it! We can put the "Night from Hell" behind us now.

We tapped for the negative statements on the Eyebrow through Top of Head points, and ended with the positive affirming phrases on the hand points. She felt much relieved and could talk about the whole incident without any upsetting emotions, whereas before she had been in tears.

Ideas for Additional Affirming Phrases to Use with EFT Setup

Even though [the negative], I deeply and completely accept myself, and…

I am willing for this to change.

I am willing to see it differently.

I am willing to accept all of my feelings without judgment.

I honor myself for facing this difficult issue.

I want to bring healing to this.

I am choosing to feel more peaceful.

I am ready to let go of _____.

I choose to know and believe _____.

The truth is, _____.

I am willing to consider that _____.

I am OK with _____.

I open myself to _____.

I am freeing myself from _____.

I honor myself for how hard this has been.

I honor all my feelings.

I honor myself for _____.

I honor the child part of me.

I honor the part of me that has been trying to protect me (help me).

I choose to forgive myself. I was doing the best I could.

I choose to forgive _____. She/he was doing the best s/he could within her/his human limitations.

Even though this _____ served me in the past, it no longer serves me.

I am sending a message to [part of the body].

I am getting through to [this part of myself].

I'm sending a message to [the child within me].

I surrender what I thought I knew for a deeper truth.

I am taking back my power; I refuse to be a victim any more.

I am letting go of my need to control _____.

I am willing to let _____ be what it is.

I am willing to consider that something good can come out of this. I can find some learning in this.

I choose _____.

I choose to feel _____.

I choose to respond with _____.

I choose to be free of _____.

I choose not to take _____ personally.

Ashe: "I Feel Like a Small Child Frozen in Fear"

(Ashe took one of my four-week teleclasses and bravely volunteered to be a tapping demonstration subject. She hadn't shared a lot of her story during the class, but since her tapping sessions over the weeks seemed quite profound and useful to her, I asked later if she would share a little about her background, and how the class had affected her. Her answer demonstrates the power of what happens to us as children, and how it shapes our adult behavior. I am so grateful for her willingness to share this. I am always honored when someone offers their story. These tales of pain and transformation become a guiding light for the healing of all of us.)

"My mother was a teacher who always played the teacher. Whatever I wanted to do, she always said I was too young. To any of my child wisdom, she would say in a derogative tone, 'What would you know? You're only a child,' even though I was proved right time and time again. I've cleared heaps around her, but nothing seems to touch this fear of doing what I am drawn to and love doing, and my fear of 'standing alone.'

"That violent crazy side of her has terrified me, and what it boils down to is I'm terrified of both doing and being, because I don't want to be like her. That started when I was very little. So I started being like my dad, which was controlling, numbing the feelings, effectively not being. Appearing calm on the outside at all costs, because otherwise she'd 'get you' energetically once she started, and then you'd end up being wrong and punished and the 'whipping post' for her to vent on.

"It required a huge amount of control not to respond, because I was so sensitive and felt all that so much. Until very recently, I always got scared around overdoing things and being tired, because I would lose my patience (read shutting down, steely tolerance, and jaw-locking self-control), and when I was little that meant being shamed big time.

"This whole thing obviously touched off something in her that scared her, too, because she couldn't deal with my reaction. Whenever I was angry, she told me I was tired. The result was that by the time I was a teenager, I got glandular fever and ended up permanently tired ... until I started clearing my anger."

A Frozen Moment of Raging Fear

"An incident with her when I was much smaller (age two to three) came up where she 'lost it' and it was so terrifying I disappeared. It was as if all there was, was her raging terror. I can see from my perspective now, that this was a frozen moment of raging fear that has been passed down the generations in my family for who knows how long. I am the first to acknowledge it, let alone deal with it. My grandmother got Alzheimer's rather than deal with her version of it.

"When I was little, my mother visited a lady who was in and out of mental hospitals, I'm sure to make herself feel sane by comparison. Nothing wrong with our family; only other people's families had problems, people who were too stupid to help themselves. My mother would go and piously try to help some poor unfortunate families!

"This is another fear. I really want to help people but *not* like that!

"All I could do with that was surrender it to a higher force, open my heart to both of us, and ask for it to be healed."

Unraveling the Knots

"Yesterday I felt very edgy, and without knowing why, I started picking on my husband and getting really angry with him. I was watching it, too. At that point, I started to notice how scared and unreasonable I was being, and I started to pay even more attention.

"It was as if a cold bony hand was gripping the inside of my stomach. I realized that having this fear and anger feeling inside her was exactly what had made my mother pick on me and tell me all the horrible things that were wrong with me. So again, all I could do in that moment was surrender it and ask for grace to open my heart to myself and her.

"I noticed some time back that I could only use my energy in defiance. That wasn't how I wanted to do things any more, but I had no way of being with ease.

"All my inner knots are unraveling nicely now as fast as I can process, and your course and EFT have helped immensely. Things just popped out so easily. It was really such a great help to work from a different perspective. I felt very safe with you.

"So this is about where I'm up to and a bit dazed by the whole thing, but open to a new way of being and doing things that I know is already there waiting for me to be ready and open to it. I've already experienced this many times, but the fear of this stuff was there, too, so I couldn't trust or love what I thought of as myself."

There are a number of themes in Ashe's story that recur throughout this book:

- Painful experiences are felt more deeply by a sensitive person, especially a child.

- Painful experiences lead to beliefs about who we are and what is possible for us in life.

- It may not be possible or safe to express the powerful anger, sadness, fear, and shame that we feel during and after these painful experiences.

- Those feelings get "stuffed" or swallowed.

- The stuffed feelings show up later in our lives as physical and emotional pain and illness.

- The people in our families who mistreated us did so because that is how they were treated, and these were the beliefs and feelings they themselves took on.

- The tendency to replicate these beliefs, feelings, and illnesses gets passed down through the generations of a family.

- The fear of confronting the powerful feelings stops us from beginning a healing journey.

- Our personal healing can heal the whole family history.

- EFT is an effective tool!

Tapping with Ashe: Borrow Her Benefits

Your life experience is, of course, different from Ashe's, but you can "borrow the benefits" of tapping along with her. Just tap along now with these phrases, as if this were your own story, paying attention to the images and memories that arise for you as you do. If something powerful comes up, feel free to pause and tap, using EFT's Basic Recipe, on the memory or emotion that you are experiencing.

Here I have taken what Ashe wrote and broken it down into tappable phrases. You can do this, too. As you consider that piercing question "What broke your heart?" choose a specific memory, as she did, and write a paragraph (or two, three, or more pages!) about it, remembering everything that was hurtful about it. Then do what I did here: Take each phrase or thought and make it into an EFT Setup phrase. Continue to do this until you can read aloud what you wrote without feeling emotionally triggered.

In the EFT Set up, after "I love and accept myself deeply and completely," I added some lovely phrases that emerged in Ashe's mind as she wrote about her tapping experience. An example is: "All I could do with that was surrender it to a higher force, open my heart to both of us, and ask for it to be healed." I began to add these phrases in her own words, feeding them back to her about halfway through, when I could sense her insight deepening and her thoughts changing as she told the story.

It is important to go ahead and be just as angry and as sad as you are at first, though, until you feel some slight changes happening inside. Then slowly begin to offer yourself some healing phrases that come from your own heart.

Near the end of the session, as you feel the opening inside, begin to change from "Even though…" to "Especially because…" to honor and enhance the flow of positive healing that is happening inside.

We used each of these statements as Setup phrases. We lifted the "problem phrase" from the statement, and tapped it through the points.

Even though I don't want to be like my mother and I am so much like her it's not funny, I deeply and completely love and accept myself anyway.

Even though I feel like a small child frozen in fear, I deeply and completely love and accept myself anyway.

Even though my mother was a teacher who always played the teacher, I deeply and completely love and accept myself anyway.

Even though whatever I wanted to do she always said I was too young, I deeply and completely love and accept myself anyway.

Even though to any of my child wisdom she would say in a derogative tone, 'What would you know? You're only a child,' even though I was proved right time and time again, I deeply and completely love and accept myself anyway.

Even though I've cleared heaps around her, yet nothing seems to touch this fear of doing what I am drawn to and love doing and my fear of 'standing alone,' I deeply and completely love and accept myself anyway.

Even though that violent crazy side of her has terrified me, I deeply and completely love and accept myself anyway.

Even though what it boils down to is I'm terrified of both doing and being, because I don't want to be like her, I deeply and completely love and accept myself anyway.

Even though that started when I was very little, I deeply and completely love and accept myself anyway.

Even though I started being like my dad, which was controlling, numbing the feelings, effectively not being, I deeply and completely love and accept myself anyway.

Even though I had to appear calm on the outside at all costs, I deeply and completely love and accept myself anyway.

Even though she'd 'get you' energetically once she started, and then you'd end up being wrong, punished, and the 'whipping post' for her to vent on, I deeply and completely love and accept myself anyway.

Especially because it required a huge amount of control not to respond, I deeply and completely love and accept myself anyway.

Especially because I was so sensitive and felt all that so much, I deeply and completely love and accept myself anyway.

Even though until very recently I always got scared around overdoing things and being tired, I deeply and completely love and accept myself anyway.

Even though I would lose my patience (by shutting down, steely tolerance, and jaw-locking self-control), I deeply and completely love and accept myself anyway.

Even though when I was little that meant being shamed big time, I deeply and completely love and accept myself anyway.

Even though this whole thing obviously touched off something in her that scared her, too, I deeply and completely love and accept myself anyway.

Even though she couldn't deal with my reaction, I deeply and completely love and accept myself anyway and I realize that having this fear and anger feeling inside her was exactly what made my mother pick on me and tell me all the horrible things that were wrong with me.

Even though whenever I was angry she told me I was tired, I deeply and completely love and accept myself anyway.

Especially because the result was that by the time I was a teenager, I got glandular fever and ended up permanently tired, until I started clearing my anger, I deeply and completely love and accept myself anyway.

Even though when I was only two or three, she 'lost it' and it was so terrifying I disappeared, I deeply and completely love and accept myself anyway, and all I can do with that was surrender it to a higher force, open my heart to both of us, and ask for it to be healed.

Even though it was as if all there was, was her raging terror, I deeply and completely love and accept myself, and anyway all I could do in that moment was surrender it and ask for grace to open my heart to myself and her.

Especially because I can see from my perspective now that this was a frozen moment of raging fear that has been passed down the generations in my family for who knows how long and I am the first to acknowledge it, let alone deal with it, I deeply and completely love and accept myself anyway.

Especially because my grandmother got Alzheimer's rather than deal with her version of it, I deeply and completely love and accept myself anyway and all I can do with that was surrender it to a higher force, open my heart to both of us, and ask for it to be healed.

Even though my mother can't admit any wrongdoing, I deeply and completely love and accept myself and am open to healing the situation now.

And so on through Ashe's story, ending with:

Especially because I've already experienced this many times, but the fear of this stuff was there, too, so I couldn't trust or love what I thought of as myself, I deeply and completely love and accept myself now, and I ask for grace to open my heart to myself.

Celia: "I Had to Carry On Like a Soldier"

(Celia, in her fifties, wrote the very first e-mail of her life to me. For many years, she had been suffering from fibromyalgia, which had put her entire life on hold. I have been deeply inspired by Celia's heartfelt and articulate words, the strength of her willingness to do EFT, and her courage to face the painful and harrowing experiences in her history. Celia is a real tribute to what is possible with EFT. I have compiled this account from some of the e-mails she wrote to me as she worked with EFT.)

"With the EFT program, I've started the Basic Recipe, starting at the very beginning of my journaling, doing three painful memories a day, starting in early childhood. I haven't gotten very far yet—again because of the pain and the fog and life's other demands. But I'm on track and working on it.

"I do have some serious issues in my life....There are a lot of bad things. The instant help you offered to me when I e-mailed you a couple of weeks ago, makes me trust that it's OK to write down the worst of it for you, though usually I keep it out of my mind. Please understand I have to treat this with a lot of reverence. It is a very long story, with much trauma both before and after this event.

"I do not like to hold this up like a 'ticket' or a 'badge' for the degree of trauma. Do you understand? I know you do.

"My fears have always been more hyper than normal. My vigilance started even before I had babies, being the oldest and watching out for the others, watching out for mom's mood swings. One attempt by an uncle at sexual molestation when I was around five, in the dark, in my bed.

"My story begins as the oldest child of a mother who suffered from serious postpartum depression, though in those days it wasn't diagnosed, and even today my mother won't acknowledge it. Her wounds were deep and that made her a distant, unhappy, and angry mother. Our reality was a serious existence punctuated by outbursts and tears from Mom and no explanations of anything from either parent.

"At some point they had agreed to not discuss their differences in front of the children, and since they disagreed about virtually everything, we grew up in a vacuum—no television, no radio, no religion, no moral guidance, no interaction between our parents and very little allowed between each other. We each lived in our own isolated little world, controlled by fear of our mother's temper and tears.

"Dad was a young dentist working for Public Health and being transferred around Canada. We moved six times in my first ten years. Mom was angry our whole childhood. She had difficult childbirths and was allergic to the anesthetic during her C-sections. Her fourth child, born when I was eight, was conceived after Mom had her tubes tied, and her anger and resentment were enormous.

"We think that she may have presumed that by marrying a young dentist she would be lifted from her prairie poverty roots to a higher level in society. Instead she ended up isolated with her ever-increasing babies, uprooted and moved almost every year for the first ten years of her marriage.

"Dad was distant, and still suffering the aftereffects of WWII. Though he wasn't physically injured, the horror of dropping enormous bombs on German cities and not knowing at which moment he and his five-man crew would become one of the planes that didn't return to base in England next morning took a huge toll on his emotional availability.

"So Mom was very isolated and angry. Instead of being elevated into higher society, she had to accept that her mother-in-law, a gentle Irish music teacher, had no interest in climbing society's ladders. My grandmother was a quiet, shy woman, busy caring for her mentally handicapped son, my dad's older brother, the surviving twin of a difficult childbirth.

"My mother's resentment was shocking. Even without television and radio to help us form our opinions, we knew that something was terribly wrong with her. Dad was old-fashioned and never spoke a bad word of her and we were taught by example to do the same. In fact, Dad's unspoken messages and disappointment with his situation (and me) possibly did more damage to my young soul than Mom's outright anger and inability to love her daughters.

"Years later, I have come to understand that much of my ability to withstand abuse came from Dad's unspoken messages that I was a disappointment, and that I had to toughen up. Part of toughening up was learning to handle Mom's outbursts. As a consequence, as an adult, when men would berate me and mistreat me it felt very familiar and deserved. I was unable to stand up for myself."

"My parents did not intentionally set out to create an icy environment for their children to grow up in. Circumstances created a difficult marriage for them and they stuck it out. Being the oldest, I was particularly aware of how cold their marriage was, especially as I got older and ventured out into my friends' and cousins' homes. Not speaking of the obvious differences in the warmth and interaction found in their homes and ours was another of Dad's unspoken laws—and we silently obeyed, other than a few teenage outbursts quickly quelled by Mom's outrage and slaps.

"Mom's hands, though gentle when we were sick (she had been trained as a nurse), were something to be feared. Somehow, for reasons we may never know, Mom's rage was her strongest emotion. It was in her hands, and for other reasons we may never know, she was unable to balance her rage with loving care.

"Writing about this now makes the little girl in me feel such loneliness and need for affection. In recent years I have had to learn how to give that little girl the loving she deserves, but of course for many years I had no idea what was wrong with me, and I became involved with men who took advantage of my need. They themselves were products of difficult childhoods and our dysfunctions brought us together, in fact, attracted us to each other and did a lot of damage to my first marriage, to me, and to my children.

"My baby Jerry (my third child) was born in March 1981, and my baby Noah was born in May 1983. Then baby Noah was killed in August 1983."

(Note: I have edited out the details of this story. It is truly horrific and none of us needs the images from it in our imaginations. In summary, Celia's three-month-old baby was killed in her arms by a rifle shot that also killed her husband. The fact that she has survived and is thriving now is such a testament to how strong the human spirit really is, how possible it is to heal from what has happened to us, and how useful EFT is as a tool to heal our broken hearts.)

"The shock of the shooting, the memories of all the violence, and trying to sort out the brainwashing and the continuing fear all combined to keep me virtually sleepless for years. I was ever vigilant. I carried on like a soldier. I'm very strong, and a lot has happened to me (more trauma). Finally, the price for being so strong was fibromyalgia and posttraumatic stress syndrome."

"EFT Has Helped!

"I am doing much better. Your set of e-mails about EFT has really helped. First, I had to deal with my body's addiction to the chemicals my brain produces when I'm in negative thinking or fear. So I put that into step one of the twelve steps and did all the steps on it. That really helped.

"Then I took 'addiction to negative thinking and fear' and put that into the tapping suggestions from you. 'I release my addiction to negative thinking and fear to my

Higher Power to transform it and my relationship to it, never to take it back or passively receive it back' and I did the tapping. I'm much more relaxed about this now and feel more like an artist than a robot doing the tapping. (Plus I'm much more gentle with myself.)

"Then I went through all the EFT points, tapping for sadness, fear, shame, embarrassment, hurt, grief, guilt, pain, anger, and trauma, then the forgiveness steps, then brought in my Higher Power to fill up the empty spaces.

"I feel a lot better. I'll keep working on this."

Celia's story is one of my favorite EFT success stories. (I have told much of her story in my book *The Eight Master Keys to Healing What Hurts*, which is available on my website, IntuitiveMentoring.com.) As a deeply sensitive person with a very troubled past, bedridden, chronically ill with fibromyalgia, and nearly an invalid, Celia began using EFT. She was very diligent, doing much of the work for herself with some guidance from me. Now she is well, employed, and strong. She went to Machu Picchu in Peru with her son last year, and climbed to the top of the mountain.

Celia understands that her health and well-being depend totally on how she thinks, feels, eats, and acts. She continues to use EFT in all of these areas. She is a living example of how effective we can be at laying new foundations for our lives, and building new structures to hold them, using EFT.

8

There Must Be Something
Wrong with Me

I got an e-mail from a young man recently, after he had read something I wrote about EFT and the highly sensitive temperament. He wrote: "Can I overcome it? Or will I be this wretch for the rest of my life? There must be some way to cure it. Moreover I think I am not highly sensitive. I love adrenaline sports, martial arts, and heavy metal and I am not pacifist or something…I don't want to live this way anymore."

He wanted to know how to tap to "make it go away." It sounds like he believes that being sensitive makes him weak, a "pacifist" (don't we need more of those in the world?). My answer to him is that his problems come not from being sensitive, but from believing that he is "this wretch." I know from what he says here that he must have been criticized and shamed for being deeply emotional and perceptive, especially as a male. He has been made to feel wrong and bad about being sensitive.

Most sensitive people, probably all of us, have had such experiences. They have broken our hearts. They have led us to create certain beliefs about who we are, how much we deserve to be here, and what is possible. Many people come to think that there is "something wrong with me." But the process actually starts even earlier, before we are even born.

Family Stories: "The Way It Is Supposed to Be"

We are born into a family story about "the way it is supposed to be." Even in the womb, we are surrounded by and absorb the effects of our mother's family story in its effects on her body, mind, emotions, and spirit at the cellular level of her body, our host. We feel the effects of our father's family story in our DNA, energetically, and in our mother's responses to him, even before our birth. If the mother is highly sensitive, her emotional responses are heightened, and if the baby in her womb has the sensitive trait, the pattern of heightened response gets laid down even more deeply. This story seems to get repeated generation after generation. How does that happen?

I came across the following description in traditional Chinese medicine. It offers a wonderful lyrical explanation for this interesting question. I call it lyrical because this explanation is not yet fully proven scientifically, or medically accepted, but it feels true. And even scientists are learning to trust their intuition. Candace Pert, a neuroscientist featured in the film *What the Bleep Do We Know!?*, says that she is beginning to operate on the "you're getting warmer, you're getting colder" rule of thumb. I love those words coming from a scientist!

In traditional Chinese medicine, the heart houses the body's spirit. Shen is the Chinese name for the body's spirit. The heart is the most intelligent and the most powerful system. The heart actually generates forty to sixty times more electromagnetic charge than any other system in the body, including the brain. Negative experiences create a disharmony in the energy system and displace the mind-body-spirit alignment. This is the "zzzzt" that Gary Craig talks about in *The EFT Manual.*

William Lieske, an acupuncturist and respected doctor of traditional Chinese medicine, states that the very first beat of our heart as a fetus in the womb begins our path as a human life. He continues:

> …The second beat, and the first in what will determine our identity, is the amygdala. The amygdala starts forming immediately after the heart's first beat. It stores all the memories of our life in the womb, with the placenta, the water, the fluids of life and the terror of losing them, and also the joy of being fed, of bouncing, of moving. But the amygdala stores also the life of the mother, her depressions, her fears, her life. And this accumulation of memories goes on in us till the age of three. Which means that all this time we have lived, our life has been recorded for us in the amygdala.
>
> After the age of three, the hippocampus matures in us. In it, conscious memories are stored and we have access to them. However, in the

hippocampus, we have no access to the memories and the life we lived in the amygdala of the previous three years, even if from this point on amygdala and hippocampus converse with each other.

What happens to the memories of the amygdala? They become our individual nightmare, the invisible conditioning of all our actions, the blind spot of our lives, the origin of all our terrors, the unknown reason why we do what we do even when we do not know why we do it...

The conditioning of the amygdala can only be removed by the intelligence system previous to it, and this is the heart, with its electromagnetic force and its power of transformation. Otherwise, the amygdala can act on its own by passing the intelligence centers of the neocortex. [Our limiting beliefs] keep acting, in spite of our good intentions.

Some of the newest developments in science add to this image. As Dr. Candace Pert and others have discovered, an abundance of vasoactive intestinal peptide (VIP) does a lot of things in the body, including creating an emotional tone associated with high self-esteem. It turns out that the developing fetus has abundant receptors for VIP but no capacity to create the substance on its own. It's completely reliant on the mother to create that. If the mother has a low sense of self-esteem, as the fetus is growing, its amygdala picks up all the fear and the low self-worth signals. The amygdala continues to record experience up through the age of three. Between ages three and seven, there continues to be an open window for the recording of experience, and especially what it means—the beliefs.

The family belief system—our family patterns of thinking and functioning in the world—lie waiting within us at the unconscious level. When we encounter a negative experience that resonates with an existing pattern, it sets off that pattern to reverberate in our lives. We grow up with those patterns in place. They act like a magnet, an energy field, that draws to us the kinds of daily experiences that will trigger the patterned responses.

So the experiences we have as children, especially as sensitive children, activate the energy patterns of the constricted beliefs that are already set in place within us. That is what cages the expression of our deepest humanity. I believe that this is what we think of as genetic inheritance. Again, I don't know if this is scientifically true in the Western sense, but it is true according to traditional Chinese medicine, and it feels true.

Experiences lead to beliefs, which lead to feelings, which when repressed or unresolved can lead to illness and pain in a highly sensitive person. This is a simple equation with profound consequences, as the following case illustrates.

Shauna: Potty-Trained at Nine Months with a Belt

(Shauna is a highly sensitive person who has fibromyalgia. Shauna's challenges began early; she was potty trained at nine months with a belt. She grew up with severe phobias, especially a phobia about not making it to the bathroom. Her mother had been pregnant with her before her parents were married, but that was a family secret that she didn't learn until she was nearly fifty.)

"The way my parents were thinking was, if I was perfect in the world's eyes, who could say anything about what they had done? The feeling from my mother was: 'You have to be what I need you to be. You can't have any needs.' So I was completely out of touch with what I wanted or needed.

"On my report card the teachers always wrote that I was painfully shy. I wasn't shy—I was extremely sensitive and I was terrified of doing the wrong thing. I didn't have friends....It is hard to have a friend if you are no one. I ended up being kind of cute and smart but serious. Man, I was one serious camper. I never felt smart enough. Never felt like a smart person. Expectations kill me. I am angry about them."

We can imagine Shauna as a little baby, long before she had words to think about this experience with, and long before she was able to look at her parents' lives and determine whether their behavior was reasonable (not that potty training with a belt could ever be considered reasonable). It is quite likely that her mother had this kind of upbringing.

It makes sense that Shauna grew up with beliefs like:

- I have to be perfect.
- I can't have my own needs.
- I am terrified of doing the wrong thing.
- I am no one.

- I am not smart enough.
- Expectations kill me.
- There must be something wrong with me.

These beliefs would have been unconsciously held, at first. As Shauna's life unfolded, she had this ready lens though which to interpret her experiences. Slowly, her unconscious beliefs emerged into her consciousness, but she experienced them as "who I am," her identity. It didn't occur to her to question them.

In her life, especially as a child, it was never possible or safe to express—or even feel—her anger. It was stuffed and buried inside, so deeply that she was not even aware of it. Eventually, her body began to hurt. As that escalated, Shauna sought medical help, and got caught up in years of seeing experts, being diagnosed, and treated with multiple drugs. Some of this treatment helped, but she didn't heal. As she said, "Expectations kill me." In fact, that can be literally true. Over time, taking on the expectations of others can actually kill us.

Tiger in a Cage: Chronic Pain Is Deep Sadness

I believe that chronic pain is a reflection of a sadness that is deep within us. It comes as a reaction to experiences that have befallen us. Our physical and emotional reaction to those experiences is a message to ourselves that we are not caring for ourselves as fully, as profoundly as we deserve.

These early experiences led us to believe that we were not worthy of attention and caring, even our attention and caring of ourselves. We began to form limiting beliefs about ourselves that slowly receded into our unconscious minds, and eventually felt so familiar that we think this is actually who we are. But our bodies carry for us all those thoughts and feelings that we couldn't, maybe still can't, speak or act upon.

Gary Craig frames working with EFT to deal with limiting beliefs as "cutting off the table legs" that hold up these beliefs, or cutting down the trees in the forest of our beliefs. Being a sensitive person, I was always a little bit bothered by the idea of cutting down forests or chopping off table legs, so I've created a metaphor that works better for me. I use the metaphor of a cage. Our limiting beliefs keep us caged in a smaller space than we can move comfortably in, but it is comfortably familiar.

I think of the story I heard once about a tiger in a zoo. It has stuck in my mind for years as a powerful metaphor of how we limit ourselves. Historically, in zoos, animals, even large wild animals like tigers, were kept in cages. Many still are, but fortunately that is changing. For the same reason I can't go to the Humane Society, I can't go to the zoo, because I always imagine being the animal that is caged, and it's too painful. The zoo of the story I heard had a huge magnificent tiger in one of their cages. All this tiger could do was pace the small space. When the tiger was given a habitat at the zoo, instead of the cage, it continued to pace the same dimensions as its old cage.

Scientists have studied animals in zoos and report that the caged animals experience the same kinds of depression, emotional illnesses, and chronic pain and immune system challenges that humans do. Thankfully, people have begun to pay more attention to how we are treating our animal co-walkers on the earth.

I think that we are like that tiger. We all have limiting beliefs that cage us. Each of the bars of the cage has been created by an experience in our lives, usually early in life, when we don't have the experience or ability to think about what it really means. As a sensitive person, exquisitely attuned to the energy around us, we may decide that that look, or that tone of voice, or how he treated me, or what she did (or didn't) do means that we are "bad," or not lovable, or not enough. When experiences like this become more and more familiar, we begin to think that they are the truth about us. The bars form all around us, and soon we can only pace back and forth within our limiting beliefs.

When the human spirit is caged or limited, it suffers. I believe that there is in all of us a deep knowing of our worth and value, and a deep love of freedom and choice, of possibility, and of creative expression. We all have adopted, typically unconsciously, a cage or two to live in. Then there is a conflict inside us. There is a difference of opinion between what we think is true and what is actually true about us that we no longer remember, or maybe never even knew because the people around us didn't know it about themselves and so weren't able to mirror it back to us. The inner conflict generates emotions of anger, fear, and sadness. We humans are like the caged tiger, living in our cages of limiting beliefs. Why would great powerful tigers like us stay in a cage?

We stay there, in our cages, pacing nervously back and forth, filled with repressed rage and grief, for lots of reasons. The cage is familiar, all we have known. It is safe. It is at least safer, we think, than venturing into the unknown.

In my first marriage, in ignorance of what was possible for me, I thought occasionally, idly, of murder, but I never thought of divorce. Divorce did not happen in my family. I would never have actually killed him of course—murder didn't happen in my family either. But looking back, I can see the power of the belief that divorce was just not an option for me. It kept me from taking action for a long time. I did take action, eventually, and I have continued to open to new possibilities in my life ever since. That experience was a profound threshold for me.

Maybe we feel helpless to act, never having had a model for having choices or possibilities. Maybe we don't feel worthy of taking action on our own behalf.

We know that people who are raised in abusive situations learn to associate love with abuse. So they unconsciously recreate what has been familiar, even if it didn't feel good, because they thought that is what love was like.

Why would any of us ever stay in a belief system that doesn't feel good? We might even ask this question more universally. The behavior of the entire human race is constantly distorted by unconscious beliefs about "the way it is supposed to be." If we thought deeply about it, we would ask: Why would people choose war as a way to solve a problem? Why would we pollute our air and water? Why would we stay in a boring soul-killing job or relationship? Why do we put up with so much pain?

The answer can only be that we don't know that is it possible to change. And we don't know that we deserve the best.

I suspect that all of our (usually unconscious) beliefs, actions, positioning, and emotions are in place as distortions and smokescreens to obscure the knowledge of our real value, even, or maybe especially, from ourselves. Our reasons for doing this may be varied, but they all add up to not feeling able to be who we really are in the world safely. It appears that all of the energy that goes into maintaining the contortions that keep unworthiness in place has the positive intention of protecting us, though the outcome may be that it kills us through the illnesses that arise from the contortions.

I have worked with so many sensitive people who, when they really looked deeply into a limiting belief or behavior, found an intention to secure peace, beauty, lightness, and love—"heaven," in other words. But the part of them that was trying to get all this goodness had very ineffective strategies. These strategies, all limiting beliefs and actions, were probably put in place long ago and certainly picked up on the way into their incarnation from ancestral family energy patterns. Those parts just kept on running the same old patterns with the same old desperation, and getting the same old results without realizing it—the tiger in the cage.

I often think of the woman I worked with who was a victim of virtually lifelong sexual and emotional abuse from her parents and later from her husband. She had a heart attack in her early forties. When she recovered consciousness in the hospital, and discovered what had happened and that she was still alive, she was thrown into an even deeper depression. She assumed that even God had rejected her, that she wasn't good enough to be in heaven and so was sent back to Earth.

But, to me, the devastation she felt said that there was a part of her that felt unbearably wounded by this thought. Her pain meant that there was an essential being-ness in her that did not believe it and thought she was worth way more than that.

Creating Cages

In my family, invisibility is one of the themes that has been handed down through the generations. My mother, a highly sensitive person herself, was a very strong, bright, creative, light-filled being. But she was aware of none of that. She never felt seen or heard, or that she existed as an active force in the world. So I grew up in that trance myself, thinking of myself as invisible.

After a long conversation with my mother once, I woke up in the middle of the night trying to think of a way of describing my mother for her home health coordinator. I was finding it hard to explain how my mother was not just the fuzzy-minded and sometimes sweet but often stubborn and cranky old lady with dementia that she appeared to be. The image came to me of a queen without a crown, a queen without a realm. I began thinking of other images that had the same sense of strong presence, but presence made invisible or obstructed: an opera singer without a voice, a wizard without a staff. I had a sense of the very intention of her life force having only a narrow, blocked channel through which to flow.

My mother had the aspect to me of someone who has great power, awareness, and wisdom, and a gracious heart, but who has seldom been able to exercise these capacities or known how to use them, or even had the assurance that they were there at all. Her two older brothers whom she and her parents idolized and favored dominated her in her growing-up years. Over time, the vitality and power in her constricted into what manifested finally as extreme passive aggressiveness, a highly critical demeanor (she was most critical of people who are critical!), and a victim mentality.

Her refrain in her life was "Nobody sees me; nobody hears me; nobody lets me finish when I try to say something." She felt herself to be the victim of others' wishes (even when she was making them up, as she did increasingly with dementia). That made her angry. But she had an unconscious belief that she could not express her anger, she could not speak up for herself, and if she did, no one would hear her anyway, and besides, no one understood. A psychologist would call this a passive-aggressive temperament.

Many years ago, I had a dramatic experience of discovering that it wasn't true that I was invisible to other people—it was that I was invisible to myself. Though my mother was never able to become visible to herself, evolving consciously into my own "Queendom" has been the story of my life. I appreciate her for letting me know so clearly through the example of her life what I could move beyond.

I'm sure my mother got her belief about her invisibility from her parents who got it from their parents, and so on, back through the generations. My sister has her own version of it. I hope my daughters will have less of that invisibility issue to struggle through. In raising them, my strong intention was to mirror their strengths, abilities, beauty, power, and essence back to them all the time. As a descendant of my ancestors, I have the opportunity to heal that wound in my ancestral spirit.

We all have limiting beliefs that imprison us, encage us. Each time you discover an experience that led to a belief that has limited you, you are removing a bar of the cage.

The wonderful value of EFT and all the other techniques of energy psychology (the relatively new field to which EFT belongs) is that each of them is good at removing bars of the cage, until soon, there is space for you to step out of the cage. And there you are, in your essential radiant sacred being-ness, visible to yourself, ready for presentation to the world in your own inimitable way.

Many good examples of the misaligned family beliefs that we are raised in come from our traditional reli-gions. This is not a rant about religion, but an acknowledgment that in some of them we can find a source for our old beliefs about our lack of self-worth, our sinfulness, and our impure thoughts, and the beliefs that arise from stuffing our emotions in response to the urgings to turn the other cheek, always forgive, and think of the other person first.

We also have beliefs about how hard and dangerous life is: It's a dog-eat-dog world; you're doomed from the start. Don't tell anyone anything; they'll have power over you if they know about you. Many people don't recognize that it's unusual or damaging to have those beliefs.

Beliefs also fall into the category of "hurry up," which is another way of saying that what you're doing is not important; what I need to have done is way more important than whatever you are doing. Or you need to do it faster, do it better, do it quicker.

"Be strong" is another belief category. This is particularly endemic among people with chronic conditions. Tough it out. Soldier on. Hunker down. Get through this. I've heard this so many times in the work I've done with sensitive people: "I just have to get through this. I can take it. I can do this." And it's true, people with chronic pain often present as being really together: well dressed, everything in place, usually very organized, and having it all together.

What are some beliefs that you picked up from your family that have held you back?

Some Spirit-Shrinking Family Beliefs

Soldier Beliefs

I have to tough it out.

…hunker down.

…soldier on.

I must suffer what comes.

Take it on the chin.

I can take it.

I just have to get through this and then things will be better.

Victim Beliefs

No one listens to me.

I'm not good enough.

I am not seen.

Self-Worth Beliefs

I'll never be as good as _____.

I am not smart enough.

This is just the way I am/just the way it is.

I have to do it perfectly (and I can't).

"Be Perfect" Beliefs

Death is better than making the wrong decision.

We don't talk about unpleasant things.

What will people think?

> **"Try Harder" Beliefs**
>
> (What you are doing is not good enough.)
>
> **"Please Me, Take Care of Me" Beliefs**
>
> (Your needs are less important.)
>
> **"Hurry Up" Beliefs**
>
> (What you are doing is not important.)
>
> **"Be Strong" Beliefs**
>
> Big boys don't cry.
>
> Oh, come on, that didn't really hurt.
>
> You're not really sick.

One person, reading the list of beliefs, wrote this to me:

I went to visit my sister and we went to her mother-in-law's house. On the wall in the kitchen was a plaque that read "Jesus First / Others Next / Yourself Last." The first letter of each word was a different style and color and when you read them down it spelled "JOY." It made me so mad I wanted to scream, but I couldn't figure out why. I've since figured it out, of course, but I was so lost at that point in my life that I couldn't even see the reason for the anger.

Stories about Family Beliefs

I asked some of the people with whom I have worked to talk about their family's beliefs, the experiences that seemed to invoke those beliefs, and what they felt they had lost as a result.

Many of the beliefs will be obvious to you. Some are implied. In either case, they can be tapped.

Norman: "The World Is a Dangerous Place"

"My parents didn't say it, but neither of them was adept at negotiating daily life or street life, the life of getting what you wanted, being aggressive in the world, though my mother was strong and insistent about what really mattered to her. Mother worried a lot; Father was kind of fearful.

"It was hard to be a boy and be sensitive at the same time. It was important in my family to be good, kind, and loving. I rebelled against this; it was difficult. I was given so many messages about being so kind and loving that I couldn't believe it. I knew I wasn't good in my heart. I lied and stole.

"We had a belief that we were smart. However, a strong belief that I have is a desire to give up, to say 'That is too hard.' People in my family were underachievers compared to a lot of other people. It seemed to me that adult life did not look that great. I was always striving to remain a boy, stay playful, avoid taking on responsibilities. My father settled into a job that didn't take much effort. It was low-key. There was no appeal to studying in school. There was not a lot of pressure to succeed in my family. Things were disorganized.

"There were some incidents of panic in my life and I became ill afterward. One was a car accident at sixteen.

I didn't get injured, but the car flipped over a guardrail at sixty miles an hour. Even a month later, I was still believing I was going to die in a car accident. So much tension built up in my body. I said to my parents, 'I am sure we are going to die in a wreck!' When we got home after the accident, I went to bed and said, 'I can't do this anymore.' I woke up sick. It felt like the flu. I said, 'I can't go to school.' I was sick for ten days. I sort of became ill to accommodate the intolerable situation of being alive. I slowly returned to normal, but after that, each time something happened that frightened me, I became physically ill afterward. If something happened that was traumatic, the fear would linger in my body and I would feel sick for days.

"But all the preceding experiences of being humiliated, hurting, and being hurt in childhood created the desire not to be seen as vulnerable. I felt vulnerable nonetheless. I hated that I was so sensitive. But at the same time, I wouldn't ever give it up."

Stephanie:
"It Would Be Better to Die Than to Have Regret"

"The main belief in my family was 'It would be better to die than to have regret.' That is, you could make the wrong decision, and if it didn't turn out well, that was worse than death. Being wrong was worse than death.

"I got the perfectionism from my dad. I would be asked to clean up the kitchen, then he would look at it and say, 'If you had done this and this, then it would have been perfect.'

"The effect of that on me as a sensitive child was that I learned to question every decision from every which way and angle to make sure that I didn't make a bad decision. I remember the day I called my parents to say I was getting a divorce. My mother said, 'Are you sure? It's really hard for a divorced woman to find another man.' You can see what her beliefs were.

"It was really hard for me to develop my own perspective and believe in and be sure of it. I would say to myself, 'It's really hot out here, but others are feeling chilly so I must be wrong.' I am always looking at everyone else from my mother's perspective, which is that my own idea isn't necessarily right. There could be a positive side to that. At work, for example, I can see both sides. But it makes you less confident and sound in who you are. How can I know what I believe?

"One of the major effects on me of my family's belief system is that I am constantly trying to avoid getting my feelings hurt. Over the years, I have learned too well from potentially dangerous and hurtful situations. I spend all my waking hours and energy trying to plan my way out of getting in those situations again. The cage gets smaller.

"One day when I was little, things were going really well and I was noticing that, then I got spanked later in the day for something I didn't know was bad. I have that as a belief now. Just when things go well, something bad happens. It is a belief in being unsafe, never knowing when things will blow up."

Gina: "My Opinions Weren't Relevant or Important"

"I was called the black sheep for as long as I can remember. I'm not sure why. That's what my mother was called in her family, too. My brothers were gods; I could never be as good as them. I must have been mischievous, maybe into everything. I was really curious. But no one took the time to do anything creative with me.

"I came away from my childhood with the belief: 'Why bother starting anything? You never finish it.' I was told, 'The only reason women go to college is to get their Mrs. It is a waste of money. They just get married and have babies anyway.' Speak when spoken to. Children are to be seen, not heard. My opinions weren't relevant or important. From the time I was a kid, I was told I was rebellious. Later on, I found out that my mother and father used to be partiers; my mother even rode a motorcycle.

"As a child, I would do things I wasn't "supposed" to do—making mud pies, typical kid stuff. My mother didn't like dirty. As a teen, I was the one who snuck out to meet my boyfriend, drank alcohol, took drugs, had sex at fifteen. My mother never said a thing. At fifteen, I made a pathetic attempt at suicide—cut my wrists. All my mother said afterward was 'Are you pregnant?' She never knew I was really unhappy. But I didn't really want to die. My father never learned of it, and never said anything to me.

"In my early twenties, I made another suicide attempt. I was really saying that I was in trouble, I needed help. I would have benefited from therapy, someone to talk to. All my mother said was 'We are not going to tell Dad.' She never got it, never asked how I was doing. My mother was an ostrich. She was so sensitive that anything she didn't want to deal with, she didn't look at. My dad was never around.

"Since I never had any encouragement, I never pursued making anything of myself. As I got older, I didn't go to college. I started working full-time. I never gave any thought to having a career. I believed my mother: women are to get married and have babies. Work was so unfulfilling and I seemed less and less likely to have babies.

"There was a lot of emotional neglect. My parents believed their role was to provide food, clothes, a roof. That was the extent of parenting. You didn't show affection, say 'I love you.' They thought you'd spoil kids if you told them too often that you love them. I didn't have any support system as a child. There were some good beliefs in my family, but they were said, not lived by."

Tapping for the Truth about You: Open Your Cage!

EFT can open the cage of your beliefs. Finding the truth about you can be as simple as reversing the old belief and adding in a mix of the positive intention, until you come up with something that makes your heart sing. People have a tendency to settle for the first way of stating a new belief that comes to mind, rather than giving it some thought and finding something that feels powerful and transformative.

Think about what could be true for you, when you become the truth of you. Be sure to reinvest your beliefs with the profound capacities that were lost in you when your painful experiences happened, such as:

- Belonging
- Being visible
- Being heard
- Feeling
- Feeling safe
- Worth, deserving
- Inner power
- Self-expression

Be sure to include the positive intention of your emotions and the symptoms of your body. What is it that they want you to know? What are they trying to get for you?

Change some of these old negative beliefs into new, wonderful, generative, exciting, fun, empowering beliefs about the real truth of your potential in the world. Ask yourself, "What would I rather believe about myself?" instead of the following:

> *"There is something wrong with me."*
>
> *"I can't do it."*
>
> *"It's impossible."*
>
> *"I could never do anything right."*
>
> *"I have the worst luck in the world."*
>
> *"I don't have a chance, so why try?"*
>
> *"I would only get hurt."*
>
> *"It would never work."*

"Whatever it is, I'd better forget about it; I just couldn't handle it."

"I wouldn't know what to do or say."

"I'd just bungle it and everyone would laugh at me."

"Who do I think I am anyway?"

"Somebody will find out who I really am and embarrass me."

"I could never do it as good as _____, so why try?"

"It's just the way I am!"

"I don't have enough information/strength/support/income."

"I might do it if I were just a little taller/shorter/stronger/faster/better."

Now, make these statements into tapping Setups. For example:

Even though I think this is just the way I am, and nothing I can do will change anything, I choose to surprise and delight myself by taking charge of my own life and making it feel good to me.

Even though I could never do anything right, I see now that I was looking through the eyes of people who were never told how wonderful and capable they were, and they were just passing on their limited worldview. I thought it was the truth! I see now that they thought they were protecting me from the cold cruel world.

Even though I came to believe that there was something wrong with me, because I never got much attention or love from them, I understand now that I might be using this pain to get attention, and that means that I am worth getting attention and being taken care of. I need to be finding fun and exciting ways of giving care and attention to myself, because they sure didn't know how to—and I do!

Let your imagination out of its cage when you do this. Write the words that describe the world in which you would want to live. Of course, just arriving at these beliefs and stating them is not enough to create actual change, although they plant really good seeds. I believe that our work is actually about healing the pain of humanity, one life at a time and one minute at a time.

This minute right here is the one for which we are responsible. That probably means that our healing is a lifelong opportunity. There may not be a simple "living happily ever after," like the fairy tales say. We tend to think of healing as a state of being, a stopped action. We think that way about peace, too. But nothing in the world ever stops. Healing, like "peace-ing," is a moving, living, breathing thing, ever changing, always responding, ever new, always emerging.

Learning our truth is about learning how to live happily ever after, even when life is not all "happy." It never is. But we can learn to live in a way that makes us feel happy, that allows us to experience happiness.

We have all heard war stories, stories of deep poverty, and even stories from the Holocaust of people finding joy and beauty in the moment, each moment. Joy in this moment creates a real possibility of finding joy in the next moment. And what is the future but a series of unfolding right-now moments? When we take care of the moment we are in right now, the future takes care of itself.

Renee: Tapping with Gandhi

My client Renee brought me a card she had made for me. It was designed around Mahatma Gandhi's wise and evocative statement:

> *Your beliefs become your thoughts*
> *Your thoughts become your words*
> *Your words become your actions*
> *Your actions become your habits*
> *Your habits become your values*
> *Your values become your destiny*

She had created an EFT tapping routine around this quote. I want to share her words with you, and then tell you how we took Gandhi's brilliant general statements and Renee's creativity and made them into a tapping routine that you can put to use right now, or any time, on something that is troubling you.

This was Renee's Gandhi EFT routine:

> *Even though most times my beliefs are negative, even though negative beliefs beget negative thoughts, I wholeheartedly accept myself the way I am, and I know there is a possibility for positive change.*
>
> *Even though negative thoughts fill my head, even though the words I use are negative, I wholeheartedly accept the way I am and I choose to believe that there is a possibility to change my thoughts and words for the better.*

Even though my negative words become physical neglect, and even though my words are mentally harmful, I wholeheartedly accept myself the way I am and I know there is the possibility for positive change.

Even though my self-harm behavior becomes habit, and even though my harmful habits feel impossible to break, I wholeheartedly accept myself the way I am. I choose to believe that there is a possibility of changing my self-harm habits.

Even though my harmful and negative habits are valuable, and even though harmful and negative habits shape my values, I wholeheartedly accept myself the way I am, and I know there is possibility for positive change.

Even though my negative values lead to my destiny in life, and even though my destiny may not be what I want it to be, I wholeheartedly accept myself the way I am and I choose to believe that there is a possibility for me to change my destiny for my highest purpose in life.

I accept that I am a person who thinks negatively, and that is that.

I loved Renee's resourcefulness. There is great value in understanding how we stitch together our lives from the fabric of the stories that we tell ourselves about what is true and possible for us.

Her statements had a touch of resignation to them, however, with the message, "Even though I know things can be different, I accept that I am a person who thinks negatively, and that is that."

I asked her to look at the first set of statements and pick a specific negative thought about herself that she would like to shift. "I guess I just don't really accept myself," she said. "I just find myself thinking negatively about myself in general."

I asked her to make a list of what she does like about herself. This isn't easy! Faced with having to come up with reasons to "deeply and completely love and accept myself," a lot of people panic. Some ways around this are to ask yourself:

- What do your parents/spouse/best friend/dog/cat/child/neighbor like about you?

- What are you good at? (from big to little things, even washing dishes, remembering birthdays, greeting the grocery checkout person, whatever you can come up with)

- What do you love to do?

Then, imagine what qualities you can elicit from the answers.

Renee first thought of being good at thinking and rationalizing. ("OK, so you are smart," I said.) She teaches university level classes about fairness and justice in the legal system. ("So you have a keen sense of equality and integrity, and you are compassionate. I can tell you are a good teacher from how you talk about your classes.")

As practitioners, we can use clients' own words to describe their values and what is important to them. In this way, we invite clients into other ways of saying—and actually meaning—"I love and accept myself." We can help people to see their own goodness without trying to convince anyone about something they don't believe, or badger them into saying something that isn't true for them. We don't have to encourage them to say something that doesn't feel true for them. This is a simple but profound concept, a delicate balance that, in our eagerness to help someone or to sound convincing, can easily be upset by our well-meaning insistence that they change their minds. Individuals can apply this same principle to their own EFT process.

With a little coaxing, Renee's list ended up looking like this:

- I can think, rationalize.
- I am smart.
- I can be intuitive.
- I can be witty.
- I can write pretty well.
- I am interested in fairness, justice, and equality.
- I like to help people.
- I look for patterns—I am good at making connections.
- I like learning/seeking/finding how things work.
- I can feel into the truth.
- I am honest.
- I am creative.
- I have a good imagination.
- I am a survivor.
- I am strong.

These statements are then woven into the tapping as counters to her entrenched and unexamined beliefs about herself. In our session, I began with Renee's negative thought, fit it into her Gandhi EFT Setups, and then picked something from her list to weave in, as follows:

> *Even though I have negative beliefs about myself, I know I have a lot of good qualities.*

> *Even though my negative beliefs have led me into thinking persistently negative thoughts, I can see that if we are to believe what Gandhi says, I can focus on some of these positive thoughts and some of my beliefs might change.*

> *Even though I haven't been able to accept myself, I do like to help people, and I am a person—what if I helped myself? I do love fairness, justice, and equality, and so maybe it is time to be more fair to myself!*

She tapped on the points, saying:

> *I can't accept myself.*
> *I don't like myself.*
> *I have a lot of shortcomings.*
> *I'm not good enough.*

(Keep tapping through all the negative thoughts and feelings you can come up with.) As Renee tapped, thoughts and questions occurred to her.

> *But what about Gandhi?*

> *He said that what you believe becomes what you think.*

What if I put my attention on some of these other beliefs about myself?

What if I use my good imagination to come up with some other things to talk to myself about besides my faults?

(Keep tapping through alternative thoughts and questions that occur to you, and alternate between these and the negative thoughts and feelings.)

Even though all my negative thinking about myself became physical neglect, and that probably contributed to the cancer and the irritable bowel symptoms, and who knows what else, I choose to believe that I can put my attention on what is good about me instead. Maybe that will help my health! Hmmm...

Even though my body has been in pain, I am wondering now if there is a connection with all the painful beliefs and thoughts that I have been feeding it. I know that there are lots of good qualities about me, and I wholeheartedly believe that there is a possibility to change my self-harming habits.

Even though I have had a habit of thinking negatively about myself, I can see that maybe that is hurting me, and maybe my body had to get that sick to get my attention. I honor myself for being strong and a survivor, and I can use my ability to learn, seek, and find out how things work to change my thought habits. What if I can help my body to work better this way?

She tapped on the points, saying:

I have been hard on myself.

I am pretty self-critical.

I have had some bad thinking habits that were turning into physical neglect.

I accept that I have been doing that.

Maybe it contributed to my illnesses.

But that is the way I learned to think in my family.

Everyone thought that way.

I thought they were right.

What if they were wrong?

What if they just never had anyone to help them to recognize bad thinking habits?

What if they thought those thoughts were the truth?

I love that I have a good imagination.

I could imagine something different for myself.

I want to be fairer to myself.

I want justice for myself!

I know that I can be creative with words. I want to find some better ones to use on my own behalf.

I am smart and intuitive.

I am a good teacher.

I can teach myself some new habits here!

What a smart thing to do!

More tapping:

Even though this persistent putting myself down has probably led to undervaluing myself, even though being so self-critical has led me to undervalue myself, I accept that I have been doing that and I take responsibility for it.

Even though being so self-critical has shaped me, and created the life I am living now, including all the illness and pain, I wonder if I could take a different shape? I know I have lots of good qualities to shape myself around.

Even though the shape I have taken has been creating a destiny that doesn't feel so good to me, and I must have thought a person's destiny was set in stone, I choose to believe that there is a possibility for me to change my destiny for my real highest purpose in life. I know I can be more. The universe will fit itself around the shape I choose to create.

She tapped on the points, saying:

I have been devaluing myself.

I have been neglecting myself—physically, emotionally, spiritually—and I see that now.

I developed some bad thinking habits, and they shaped my values, my choices, even my self-value.

I neglected myself.

I like making connections and I can understand what I was doing now.

That self-criticism was just my thoughts! It isn't the truth about me!

I really am a smart, intuitive, strong person.

I am honest. Honestly, I deserve better treatment from myself!

I am going to be more honest about my good qualities.

Hey, honesty is the best policy!

I have always wanted to know my purpose in life.

Maybe I have some clues here — what if my purpose is to change the way I think about myself? That would change everything!

By changing my thoughts, I could change my health.

By changing my thoughts, I could change my destiny!

What if Gandhi was right?

If my destiny is not turning out the way I want it to be, I can change my thoughts and change my destiny! It is up to me!

I like how that thought feels.

I deeply and completely accept this possibility for positive change.

I have always been creative. I can create a new destiny for myself!

I have a good imagination.

I can imagine myself right into my highest purpose in life.

Changing my thoughts about myself is my highest purpose.

In a recent session with another woman who was tapping along in a similar vein, she suddenly burst into tears. "There is a whole other part of me that I never saw!" she cried. "And it has been here all the time." We had to do a little tapping about deserving that, but since that part of her was her, and had been all along, there wasn't much debate in the end.

Try this Gandhi tapping protocol for yourself. Adjust and change it as it feels right to you. Change the story of *your* life!

9

I Have to
Tough It Out

I have heard various versions of the phrase "I have to tough it out" from countless sensitive clients. HSTs are so good at being the strong one, the competent one, the dependable and reliable one. We have had to learn how to do that because, in the past, it may not have been possible or safe to express what we were actually feeling. Or maybe being the "go to" person seemed like the only way to get some approval. HSTs try so hard.

So many sensitive people have just learned to swallow what is inside us, stuffing down the words, the tears, and maybe even the joy and excitement. It was all too much. We locked away inside of us our true desires for what we wanted. We taught ourselves not to want. We taught ourselves to think that what we wanted was what they wanted us to want. This left us stuck in a gray world of "should" and "have to" and "better not" and "I am all alone here." We thought we had no choices.

Here are some stories from people who grew up learning how to "tough it out."

A Freudian Slip: "I Love and Except Myself"

(The following is from an e-mail from Celia, whom you met in chapter 7.)

"Dear Rue, I am remembering parts of our phone session, especially trying to learn to say thank you if someone compliments me, instead of cringing in cynical disbelief. Also, the conclusion that I need to tap (probably a lot and for some time persistently) on disconnecting my present-day reactions from those instilled in me by my mother's very negative input and those instilled in me by abusive men who used violence to frighten me into obedience (a continuation of how I was treated as a very young child).

"I want to learn to grow my stronger side and learn to disconnect from the part of me that is so easily frightened and cowed into a subservient, submissive posture. I have to honor that sensitive little girl who was unable to stand up to the dominance and beatings of my baby self, and honor the sensitive adult woman who also caved in under threats, physical violence, and enormous fear. I have felt weak and ashamed for so many years—it's hard to make the shift to positive and proud.

"The best shift that happened while I was talking to you came when we were tapping and you were able to coax me to say out loud, 'I am of value' and then even 'I am of great value!' I was surprised by how sure of that I was—the sureness came from deep inside—and I am certain that it is a result of the EFT work I have done over the last few months, especially gently rubbing over my heart and saying, 'I deeply and completely love and except myself.' What a gift this is. I can feel God teaching us all about love. How lucky we are.

"Do you have any ideas of a tapping sequence to help me release my mom's damage to me? I can use your visualization of a tree with the patterns of damage caught in the branches (thinking) and roots (past), and fit in 'mom's damage to me,' and then release all the negative emotions connected to that one at a time, and persistently."

In a reply to Celia, I pointed out the Freudian slip of "I love and except myself." How appropriate a mistake for someone who had believed that she has no value!

Later Celia wrote another e-mail:

"Young Soldiers Have to Toughen Up"

"Today I thought my way through to understanding that from a very young age I knew two things from my dad: that I was a disappointment and that young 'soldiers' have to toughen up. So two things developed in me at the same time: an acceptance that I deserved to be thought poorly of and a toughness to carry pain, 'keep my chin up,' and not fight back against the commander — Mom.

"My dad's war experience cut him off from his own sensitivities and he saw his children's frailties as weaknesses. So now I understand better why I have trouble recalling my buried anger directly related to mom's treatment of me. I thought I deserved it and that I had to learn to be tough. It wasn't until I was a teenager that I began to feel anger, but even that was mainly about Mom's treatment of others, not me.

"So the origins of my low self-esteem (and the fibromyalgia) are buried very very deep. Whatever anger I may have felt and buried as a very young child was pushed down even further by the certainty that I was a bad girl and deserved (more than the other children) to be treated poorly, and that my ability to accept that treatment meant I was becoming a good little soldier. No wonder I have trouble recalling anger over how I was treated, but no trouble recalling anger over how the rest of my family was treated. That was so interesting to me just how blank I was when you asked me specifically to recall my own personal anger over how I was treated. I'm onto it now though, and will work on getting some tappable phrases figured out. Thank you, thank you!

"Here are what I found to be tappable phrases about my father's involvement in my ability to stuff my anger way down deep into potential fibromyalgia territory. I haven't tapped on them yet, but when I do, I'll let you know how it goes. I am so looking forward to breaking out of all this into the light. I know I'm already well on my way.

Even though [each of the below], I deeply and completely love and accept myself and am open to healing the situation now.

My dad treated me like I was a disappointment

My dad treated me like a young soldier who had to toughen up

My dad taught me to accept that I deserved to be thought poorly of

My dad taught me how to be tough

My dad taught me to keep my chin up and carry the emotional and physical pain

My dad taught me not to fight back against Mom

My dad saw his children's frailties as weaknesses

My dad's war experience cut him off from his own sensitivities

I have trouble recalling my buried anger directly related to Mom's treatment of me

I thought I deserved it and I had to be tough

The anger I felt was pushed very far down inside

The origins of my low self-esteem are buried very deep

My anger was pushed down by the certainty that I was a bad girl

My anger was pushed down by the certainty that I deserved to be treated badly

My ability to accept that treatment meant I was becoming a good little soldier, which won my dad's silent approval

"Time to get tapping on this!"

Silvia: Toughing It Out by Perfectionism

"I have a very sensitive temperament and sensitive body. I feel that my body is betraying me. It is not cooperating. There are things I want to do and it is not cooperating.

"During college I decided that overachieving was fun. I thought if I worked harder I could get straight A's. Then I decided if I could take heavier course load and still get straight A's, it would be an even bigger achievement. Then I went on to finish my degree in two years nine months. I graduated on the dean's list. My senior year is when the migraines started.

"Achieving high results felt really good, but there is a piece that what I do is never good enough. It goes back to the perfectionist thing.

"In my family, it was about never getting a lot of praise for doing well. The refrain was 'You can do better, you can do better.' I am continuing to try to get that praise. Who am I trying to get it from now? Everyone I can. Trying to get it from myself.

"My first symptoms seemed to be more a food-related trigger. Maybe it was actually from underlying stress. Normal work kind of charged me up, but then things would start humming at a higher rpm. I would get irritable bowel syndrome episodes. I reacted to fried potatoes, high-fat foods, mayo, and cream-based soup.

"The next ratchet up was work-incident stress. I was planning work inventories; there were pressures, expectations, demands, change, requests. It was very stressful. My hair was falling out in gobs. I was diagnosed with TMJ [temporomandibular joint syndrome]. Then I went to the chiropractor; he diagnosed it as back problems. The doctor diagnosed it as sinuses. Now I know it was fibromyalgia. Whatever muscles I last stressed got stuck. Whenever I was diagnosed by a specialist, they said I had whatever they treated.

"The next ratchet up, I got a job that was very political, and it required me to travel a lot. There were long days, debating, late dinners, trying to sleep, my mind spinning, trying to reason out the arguments. I ended up with more jaw pain, headache, pain in my back, more sleep problems.

"I took a different job, and then I found a lump in my breast. It was breast cancer. I had chemo and radiation, and that took stress up to the next level.

"I think the beliefs behind all these physical symptoms stem from perfectionism. In my twenties, I had more balance, but now my cage feels like it is getting smaller; the balance is tipping the other way. I used to like to socialize, but I know from past experience that I will have pain. My world is getting smaller.

"There is always this sense in me that there are unwritten rules that I don't know about. That's hard; you lose your zest for life, your ability to take it in and enjoy it, just do it and not think about it. I always have to analyze-plan-reflect-figure. There is no spontaneity, no trust in my own instincts.

"There is also not being revealing. I am not a very revealing person because I don't want to put myself out there, don't want to get hurt. But this way, you end up not really fully being you, I think.

"There is always a question: Did I do something to bring this on? Could I have avoided it? Could I have planned my way around it so it wouldn't happen? In my family, if you made a mistake, someone would say, 'I guess you should have thought of that.'

"I do that to myself all the time: What is wrong with you that you didn't think of it? I beat myself up, but it's more tied into thinking that if I'd thought of it, I wouldn't be in this hurtful situation. I didn't apply enough energy, didn't think enough. I do that kind of thinking twenty-four hours a day, even when I am supposed to be sleeping.

"My planning mechanism is in overdrive. The more pain and other symptoms, the more you have to plan in order to work around avoiding a spiral into an un-winnable situation. It is hopeless. My way is to plan, plan, plan, but I'm always one step behind.

"Earlier in my life I was quite charged up about my life. Lately, it's negative. My analogy is those little merry-go-rounds at the playground, where you push on the bars and run, hop up, and ride for a while till it slows down. When it works like that, it's fun. But if you run and push it and lose your footing, you have to hop up onto it or fall down and hurt yourself. I feel now like I am running and running and can't get my feet under me, but if I let go, I will get hurt. If I can just run a little harder, I can get my felt under me again. If I let go and roll…but I can't quite get myself to risk the pain. I am presuming that I can get my feet under me again. Do you think I am wrong?"

Tapping for the "Shoulder Soldiers"

One of the tapping volunteers in a teleclass said that she felt the pain of a belief in her shoulders, which she described as "a sharp red burning pain in my shoulders that radiates to my arms and my skull." We began to tap for this red burning pain in her shoulders, and at one point as she repeated the phrases, she accidentally said "the burning red pain in my soldiers." That caught my attention! I visualized all these tough, hard-working, exhausted, confused, hurting red-coated soldiers in her shoulders. They extended into her arms and her neck, working too hard, carrying burdens, often feeling events that happened to her as a "pain in the neck."

I began to wonder out loud as we tapped through the points about all these "shoulder soldiers" who had been working so hard all these years to carry the burdens she felt. She said, "It is very difficult for me to ask for support, or to admit weakness, failure, or mistakes. This causes a lot of stress and also isolation."

We tapped. I offered some phrases and invited her to speak up with phrases and ideas that were occurring to her. We often stopped to check in with the feeling in her shoulders and her neck. Sometimes we would begin in a new direction with the same issue as it came to us. The following is a much shortened version of the flow of our tapping through the points:

Soldiering on has gotten really old...I'm ready to stop fighting...but those soldiers were protecting things...Without that protection, I'm feeling all kinds of stuff all of a sudden and it's overwhelming...it's really painful...it's a pain in the neck...my arms hurt...I can't reach out for help...and being overwhelmed, I don't know where to start...All these overwhelming emotions...the feeling I have to do it all on my own...all this sadness...all this anger...I can't ask for help...I don't value myself enough to ask for support...I feel like I'm just one big ball of pain all of a sudden...My defenses are down and all I do is cry…but I'll be rejected if I cry…I don't even want to do EFT.

At one point, I felt a little stuck in our tapping process, sort of untethered out there in space with her valiant shoulder soldiers, but needing to bring the session to a reasonable stopping place since we were nearly out of time. As so often happens for me, I sent out a little request to the Universe for help here and was suddenly struck with a thought. This was a woman who said she couldn't reach out for help, and here she was sharing her own deep feelings with an unseen but very present group of more than two hundred people. There was an implicit invitation to this community of co-tappers to create a "network of holding" and a powerful intention in their own hearts that she, and all of us, might find ways to heal this issue. We all wanted the best for her! It was making us feel good to be asked for help!

In the wonderful magic of EFT tapping, the concept of Borrowing Benefits suggests that we all gain benefits in working through our own problems when we tap together as a group. There is science to back this up.

So I began to weave in words about all of us being together in a common mission to heal each other, and by extension to heal the heart of humanity. Part of me was thinking that maybe this might too "spacey" a concept for some people, but a stronger part of me could feel the powerful effect that was flowing through the group, and especially through the volunteer tapper. I trusted that. Her voice tone was changing, her verbal responses were changing, and I could hear sighs and yawns, which indicate a release of energy coming from inner transformation.

Asking for support can foster loving connections. After the class, this is what this volunteer wrote to me:

> I am really glad I didn't know beforehand that there were so many people listening in, but I also think that added to the power of the session for me. It was quite a big step for me to stay present with so many "observers," as I generally suffer from performance anxiety in a big way, and have a habit of going blank in those kind of situations.
>
> My shoulders are a lot easier than they've been in years. Some of the stuff around not being able to be strong and ask for support at the same time is really important. I've never connected that so clearly before, so it's been either "shouldering" on alone—that one is going to be a classic—or making myself weak and disempowered.
>
> The other really important insight for me has to do with the mission, or maybe rather purpose, of creating connections and opportunities for mutual love through asking for support. That possibility is truly a revelation to me, I need to work a bit more on that one! I'm glad you're continuing with the "toughing it out" theme; that's juicy stuff.

Using the Story Map to Tap for "Having to Tough It Out"

In order to develop a big picture of the issue, I often ask people to complete the Story Map (see chapter 5). It tells the story of the belief that they carry about themselves, and it offers some insight about how it came to be in place in the person's life story. The Story Map produces many tapping phrases that can be woven through the session. You can do this for yourself, or for someone else. It can be emotional and healing in itself for the "toughing it out" issue to fill in the blanks in these sentences.

I have to tough it out because _____.

A belief/behavior/outlook on life/self-image about toughing it out and soldiering on that I got from my family is _____.

That has created a problem in my life because (or when) _____.

That made me feel _____.

It made me think I was _____.

I feel that in my body here: _____ [name part].

Some of the beliefs about toughing it out and soldiering on that are common:

I have to be tough. The world is a tough place.

It is up to me. No one will help me.

It is weak to ask for help. I will be hurt if I ask for help.

_____ is my fault, so I have to be perfect to make up for it.

If I cry, they will call me a crybaby and shame me.

I can't show what I am really feeling—that makes me too vulnerable.

I don't deserve support.

I have to prove that _____.

Some of the feelings that come up around these beliefs are anxiety, sadness, fear, depression, and anger or feeling vulnerable, crazy, alone, helpless, dismissed, guilty, unworthy, and trapped. The physical symptoms of these often unconscious beliefs are wide ranging. Clients have reported chronic nausea, " a gripping feeling in my center," "a square block of tension in my back," "My heart hurts," "My chest and throat ache," "My legs feel weak and I am off balance," "I can't breathe," and "something heavy sitting on my chest."

The beliefs, feelings, and physical symptoms lend themselves naturally to Setup statements:

Even though I think I have to be tough because the world is a tough place, and you only survive if you have a hard enough shell, I accept myself anyway, and I honor myself for how difficult this has been.

Even though I can't cry because that makes me look weak, and they will make fun of me like they did when I was growing up, I love, accept, and appreciate myself for finding a way to survive.

Even though I honor other people's trauma more than my own, I realize that my chronic nausea is telling me that I am literally sick of ignoring my own trauma. I accept that I have been living this way and I am now choosing to pay attention to what I need.

These beliefs are so powerful in our lives because we grew up in the midst of them. We didn't think to question them. Our parents probably believed something similar, and they unconsciously thought they were doing us a favor by making us tough so that we would survive, just like they did. That means that someone taught them that the world was a hard, unforgiving place, and those people learned it from their parents as well. When we heal these old unexamined beliefs in ourselves, we are healing the heart of humanity.

10

Stuffed Feelings—
EFT for What You Couldn't Say

Often in EFT sessions, I ask people the question, "What did you want to say that you couldn't?" Highly sensitive people typically grow up having to put a lid on their expressive spirit all the time. They hear, "You're too smart for your own good," "too loud," "too talkative," "too energetic," "too much imagination," "too dreamy," too adventurous," "too honest," "too intense," just "too much" in some way. When the parents or teachers around them got upset with how "out there" they were, they began to shut down, thinking that there must be something bad about being who they are.

Because connection is so important to sensitive people, they denied their own truth in order to maintain connection with others through the other's approval. In addition, it was unsafe for many to express what they really thought and felt. As discussed throughout this book, that becomes a way of life and an identity, and their own truth gets buried. Those stuffed feelings can later show up in emotional or physical pain.

Here are four examples of tapping sessions that dealt with the question, "What did you want to say but couldn't?"

Lisa: "Clenching My Jaw So I Wouldn't Talk Back to My Mother"

Lisa started our session one day by telling me how much better she was doing since our last session. The pain and cramping that had made her hands "stuck closed" had loosened up now. But then she began to describe how the pain seemed to be moving up her arms into her neck, where it used to be, "a sharp, burning pain."

I asked her when she first started noticing pain like this. She talked about thirty years earlier when she had such terrible tension in her jaw.

I imagined her jaw clenched closed, and the question popped out: "What did you want to say back then, or even earlier in your childhood, but couldn't?"

The answer wasn't on the surface for her yet. Tapping on the side of her hand, she mused out loud until she got to it: "There was something in my mind all the time back then. I kept thinking, 'I can't wait to get out of childhood, I can't wait to get out of my family.' I wanted to scream, 'Let me out of here! This is a crazy place. I don't belong here!'" Then she said in surprise, "You know what? I was keeping my mouth closed so I wouldn't say that to my mother. And I wanted to ask 'Why are you hitting me?' I had to control myself so I wouldn't ask why when she said no, you can't ride your bike, go for a walk, play outside.

She always said no. When I did ask her why, she said, 'Because I said so.' I had no voice."

I had been scribbling furiously as she said all this, and now we had lots of EFT Setup statements that cycled around, wanting and needing to say something and not being able to say it.

As we tapped, she was easily able to make the connection with situations in her life ever since then, when she had something to say that was her own, but she didn't say it. In fact, she had only recently escaped from a marriage in which she had no voice, and now found herself in a relationship in which she could see herself falling into the same pattern, though she was now well beyond the helpless person she had been earlier in her life.

During the tapping, Lisa felt waves of tension sweep through and out of her jaw. By the time we finished, her jaw was relaxed and open. Now she could feel, with strength and clarity, what she wanted to say to her current partner.

Deirdre: "My Throat Contracted Around My Sadness"

Another time that I popped this question was when Deirdre was talking about the dreams she was having.

"Lately all my dreams have a theme of 'Pay attention to me,'" she said. She was feeling as if there was a child part of her that she hadn't acknowledged, that there were "feelings inside that I am not feeling—they are stuck in there."

I asked her just to use her imagination and start talking. What could this be about? Often a person says they don't know what is going on, but when I say, "Just pretend that you do know," they start talking and something almost always emerges that is a revelation for both of us.

Deirdre, thirty-five, has a job that is OK but doesn't really tap her creativity and intelligence. She said, "Well, I have always had a hard time in my life knowing what I want to do. I am always carried along by others' expectations. I feel scared of listening and finding out what I want."

This last sentence jumped out at me. I asked, "Where in your body do you feel that 'scared of finding out what I want' feeling?" Often when we give our attention to something that we have been avoiding, it just naturally begins to open out. Giving our attention to the physically held aspect of the feeling is safer than approaching it directly as an emotion or memory.

"I feel it a lot in my throat—it's tight," she said. "It is like there is a lot of heavy sadness stuck in my throat. My throat is contracted around this sadness. It wants to come up and out, but my throat doesn't want it to come out."

"What if you let it up and out?" I asked. "What would happen?"

"Oh, I would make a horrible sound. My head might explode. I couldn't control it!" she exclaimed.

We began our tapping right there, with the sensations in her throat and the sadness. To make this a safe experience for her, I invited her to imagine that there was an ally in her own belief system—a real person, an angel, a mythical figure—that could hold her safely while she tapped, so that her throat could open. Inspired by Caroline Myss's Archetype Cards, she chose the Angel archetype as "a strong, serene, supportive presence that could guide me and protect me through it." I asked her to build an image of this presence, and how it felt to be held by it. Then we tapped.

She realized that this strong painful sadness came from feeling abandoned as a child. She had been holding this deep pain in since then. Her throat had been closed around the fear of feeling this pain. Now that she had been alerted by her dreams, and knew what they were about, she knew that she could handle working with the issue with EFT.

Debra: What Are You Trying to Cough Up?

Debra (it just happened that these examples are all women, but they could just as easily have been men) called to say that she wanted to cancel the session because she had a terrible cough that was draining her energy. She felt exhausted all the time. She had actually had this cough for many years, she told me, but it was particularly bad right now. She had an appointment the next day to see a doctor about her hypothyroidism.

Instead of canceling, we worked on the cough.

Since her call, I had been thinking, "What are you trying to cough up?" Right away, I asked my question. Her answer turned up something interesting. Her issues came down to this:

"I didn't have any right to have an opinion, even though I knew inside that my opinion was right. My mother punished me for saying what I thought if I disagreed with her. But when I think of it, my grandmother never was able to say, or even know, what she thought. This issue must go way back in my family."

Long story short here, it turns out that in naturopathic medicine, the thyroid reflects a person's voice in his or her life. When the voice "feels trapped," over time, the accumulated effect gives rise to symptoms that can include poor thyroid function. It makes sense that holding in and repressing one's truth can result in the physiological symptoms of severe fatigue and loss of energy, weight gain and difficulty losing weight, depression and depressed mood, joint and muscle pain, and headaches.

We tapped on her cough. We tapped on several specific events in her life around the time that the cough began to show up, times when she had felt that someone was trying to "kill me emotionally" and she hadn't felt able to speak up for herself. It wasn't long before she said, "Now I know I have a right to see things my way, and I have a right to have an opinion!"

Patsy: "I Didn't Have a Right to My Own Opinion"

Patsy was telling me how much better she had been doing lately. "My self-talk is much more reassuring," she said. I asked her for some examples.

"My self-talk says, 'Slow down. Do one thing at a time. Do what you can do. You don't have to do it all right now.' I am slower to get annoyed or irritated with myself. I understand myself better now. The only thing I am not so good at is letting go of all the shoulds. In fact, it has been kind of a big plus for me to have the disease I do."

Patsy had Crohn's disease. Statements like her last one are a huge red flag for me. They signal that some body condition has become part of the client's identity and is performing a function for her that, inside, she thinks she cannot perform for herself, for whatever reason. The equation goes like this: Physical condition = sabotage of healing in order to protect myself.

I asked Patsy what she meant by "big plus."

She said, "If you eat wrong or hold emotional things in, the disease flares up. It gives me the power I don't have on my own to say no."

"So, Patsy," I asked, "Who, in your past, could you not say no to?"

"I couldn't say no to my mother. Her routine was always 'Mother knows best.' She made my life miserable. I had a very close relationship with her when I was little, but the cost was in saying no to me in order to say yes to her. I tried, I argued with her, but that got me in a lot more trouble. It was just easer to give up, give in."

To work with this sabotaging setup with Patsy, I mapped the information so it would all be right there in front of me as we tapped. You can create your own map. Think of some interesting and easy-to-remember shape that has several points, each of which can be a gathering place for certain information. I use a stick figure of the human body. We chose a situation in Patsy's history that illustrated the issue of saying no and the reaction triggered in her body. I recorded notes on the stick figure as follows.

Notes below the stick figure:

We gave the situation a title: "Mother Knows Best."

Under that I wrote her statement, "I had to say no to me in order to say yes to her."

Notes at the stick figure's right hand:

The <u>feelings and emotions</u> were anger, discomfort, and sadness. These feelings were triggered by the snide tone in her mother's voice and the look on her mother's face. Translated into words, they mean, "You are so wrong," "I hate you for your choice," and "You shouldn't want this; you should want what I want."

Notes at the stick figure's left hand:

The <u>symptoms and behaviors</u> in Patsy were: "a clenching feeling in my stomach and my chest that moves across my collarbone," "a feeling of bracing myself," "My shoulders feel like they are weighted down," and "I am waiting for confidence to magically descend."

I pointed out the interesting fact that the word "shoulders" has the word "should" in it, and there is the evocative play on words in "wait/weight," all of which can be woven creatively into the EFT wording.

Notes at the stick figure's head:

The <u>beliefs</u> that arose from the experience were:

- I don't have a right to my own opinion.

- What I think doesn't matter.

- I have no power.
- I am not good enough.

Notes above the stick figure's head:

The <u>positive intentions</u> of the emotions were:

- My anger and sadness want me to acknowledge that I am a person in my own right.
- I am free to think for myself.
- It is OK for me to want what I want.
- I can express my own opinion and still be loved and supported.
- I can say yes to me!

Together we tapped for all of these emotions, symptoms, and beliefs. For me, one of the good things about having all these words and phrases right in front of me in my map is that it stimulates my intuition and my creativity. I find myself riffing off of unusual combinations of these words and concepts in a way that is fun to do, and often funny. It is a good thing to laugh in the midst of a serious EFT session!

I concocted various takes on "Mother Knows Best" at one point, playing with:

- Mother Nos Best.
- How good do *you* want to be at no-ing.
- The No's of Truth.
- Your own opinion is as clear as the "no's" on your face.
- I should no better.

- I can and do no better now!
- I can carry on my own shoulders what my Self knows about my "no's!"

Probably some even better ones are occurring to you right now.

We completed the tapping session by tapping in all the positive intentions. I used a similar creative weaving style, sometimes with humor, but more often with the intention of grounding Patsy's own sincere, powerful sense of presence and truth.

Now when she looks back on her life, she can recognize that this sense of rightness and strength and trust in her Self has always been there. I invited her to remember specific times where she could notice that this is true. She has always had an opinion and a voice, and now she knows she can trust it.

Christine: "It Wasn't Safe to Be Happy"

In my EFT teleclasses, we regularly experience remarkable deep work, as members of the group take on and transform deep-seated beliefs that have caused ongoing physical and emotional pain. This was the case recently for Christine, a forty-year-old woman of Chinese ancestry.

Christine worked gracefully with a constricting belief from her ancient cultural tradition about the role of women in maintaining family harmony and (therefore) national harmony. With EFT, she found a way to step in a new healing direction as an individual woman, while maintaining honor and respect for her group heritage.

Tap along as you read, and borrow her benefits like the rest of us did during the class! This is almost the transcript of the whole session, so you can see how it evolved. It is long, but full of useful ideas for the practitioner and for anyone who has a limiting belief. (Know anybody like that?)

In this session, we used my Take a Stand protocol. I developed this powerful tool for using EFT to help people to transform old, no longer useful beliefs that are in conflict with other, expanding parts of us. It involves creating an imaginary circle on the floor. The person begins by standing at the bottom of the circle, and takes steps around the circle with each change.

We Embody What We Believe

I always start by asking the client how his/her body holds the belief with which he/she wants to work.

Christine began by saying, "Every time I am grateful for my life, or feel particularly happy, or focused on something wondrous that I love (that is not related to work or family or anything that is considered acceptable to be focused on by my family), I sabotage myself. I am not able to stop this veil that just comes down and make everything feel flat, or I hear a voice say 'You can't be that happy! It's not safe to be happy!' or some part of me points out what was imperfect. I would be surprised and submit to this voice. I am stumped at this unhappiness.

Sometimes it feels like self-hatred. I feel it as a tightness in my chest."

My attention was caught by her feeling that it wasn't safe to feel happy, especially about anything her family didn't consider acceptable.

We embody, in our physical bodies, what we believe. We can notice how we tighten and constrict around a belief that makes us sad or angry. When we open to a belief that feels freeing to us, our bodies feel light and buoyant. Our bodies and our feelings are our best guidance!

So we began with Christine standing up and feeling into how her body represented this belief. Her chest felt heavy and tight, her throat was clenched up, and she had a "crying with no tears" feeling. The emotions she felt were sadness, anger, and fear. Her head was down, her shoulders rounded, and her weight was back on her heels.

She said then, "I am afraid that if I change, I will leave everything I know behind."

We began to tap for the belief that "If I change, I will leave everything I know behind, and that is very frightening," and the feelings it evoked. I kept suggesting the phrases that came to me, encouraging her to embroider, replace, or elaborate on what I said, with her own thoughts and feelings. Christine's intensity, which had started high, was going even higher. We wove in and out of a kind of tapping conversation:

> *Even though I am afraid of my fear, afraid of my feelings — there are too many feelings involved here — I'm open to thinking differently about my feelings.*

Even though I am afraid of my anger, I accept myself anyway. Even though I am afraid to change, I accept that I feel this way—there is a message for me here.

While we tapped together on the points (I have the client tap on his/her body and I tap along on mine), I said:

Afraid of my anger...afraid to heal this...I'm angry with myself for wanting to heal this...I don't want to heal this...Yes, I do...No, I don't, it's too scary...It makes me angry that I want to heal this...I feel such conflict...I want to heal this thinking...but if I heal this thinking I'm afraid I will lose a lot...Part of me is angry that I want to change...I'm afraid I'll have to leave what I love behind...This feeling in my chest...clenching in my throat...part of me saying no, part of me saying yes...maybe another part of me is spelling that a different way...

"What?" Christine said at this point. "I am confused!"

I continued:

Part of me is saying yes, part of me is saying k-n-o-w...I wonder what the message is for me here? What does this conflict want me to know?...All this fear...all this crying without tears, all this anger...Who taught me to feel this way? How did I learn to keep feeling that way, and prevent myself from changing? Who told me I couldn't be happy?

I suggested that Christine tap on the side of her hand while she asked that question of herself, and to notice what came up. "What happened in childhood when you did something good? Who gave you that idea that 'I shouldn't be happy—it's not OK for me to be happy?'"

"My stepmother," Christine said.

I responded, "When you think about her message to you, how did you learn from that interaction? What is it that stands out as you think about it now? Was it her words? The tone of her voice? Her gestures? The look in her eye? What was it that gave you that message?"

"I see her eyes," said Christine.

How would you describe the look?

"Full of hatred."

She tapped:

Even though I have this memory of "it's not OK to be happy, not OK for me to be happy," and that was the message in my stepmother's eyes, and I believed her, and I have believed her ever since, I believed she could kill me...

Even though I believed that she could kill me with that look, I love and accept myself anyway.

Even though I was terrified of that look in her eye and I took on her belief that it's not OK for me to be happy, that if I am happy something bad will happen, and I have held this belief since I was eighteen and maybe longer, there is a part of me that knows that I deserve better.

We tapped for the look in her eyes, the message in her eyes, the feelings. The intensity was starting to go down now. At one point in the tapping flow, I said, "I had to take on her thinking in order to survive," and as we tapped with that phrase, Christine caught herself in a verbal slip. She heard herself say instead, "I hate to take on her thinking." We wove this in, working with the idea that she had to agree to her stepmother's thinking in order to keep the harmony, but it wasn't right for her. She hated feeling forced to keep a harmony that felt poisonous to her.

She tapped:

Her thinking is toxic...it's poisonous to me, poisoning me...but I had to take on her thinking in order to survive...This terrible conflict...I have been living this conflict for much of my life...I wasn't allowed to have my own thoughts because I had to keep the harmony...and that is important in my culture...I want to honor my culture, but I want to honor myself as well...I deserve to honor myself...How can I honor myself and still have harmony?

I asked Christine to stop and breathe, and feel into what was happening inside.

She said, "Now I am feeling sad that this was my conflict, and that I couldn't articulate it. Anger that I had to put up with this. Glad I can articulate it now. Hope that we can go with this. I have been tapping a long time about this issue but hadn't gotten to this level of clarity."

Doubting and Wondering: Is That Really True?

Now I asked Christine to begin wonder and doubt about that old belief that it wasn't OK for her to be happy. I was asking her to imagine that she could point herself toward a healing direction, without insisting that she choose some new belief just yet. I wanted her to give herself permission to feel her thinking becoming less constricted and more fluid.

Christine stood up again, and stepped from the old belief to a place of doubting and wondering. She let her body take on a "thinking about/wondering" position. She cocked her head, cupped her chin in her hands, and looked up, her weight on one hip.

She had talked about feeling powerless, so I asked, "What is an area of your life that you have power in? Or when did you do something well? How did you tune into your feeling of power at that time?"

She described a situation, and then said about it: "To run away was my first strategy. Of course that didn't work. I felt powerless, so I went inside and asked my soul what there was for me to learn in this. I got the answer, 'Forgiveness.' I asked my soul, what would it feel like to forgive? 'A happy feeling' was the answer. I stayed with this feeling. I ended up appreciating this person. I had never experienced forgiveness this way. I just stayed with the feeling of happiness, not the words about forgiveness. I didn't have to do anything; the bad situation just unraveled."

We tapped:

Even though I used to believe it's not OK for me to be happy, and I have believed that for a long time, because my stepmother was a very powerful person, I am wondering now what would it be like to ask my soul about my power.

Even though I have believed for many years that it is not OK for me to be happy because of that message in my stepmother's eyes, I am open to wondering if that is still true for me.

Even though part of me has believed all of my life that it's not OK for me to be happy, I am open to wondering if there is any other truth here. What if I asked my soul what it would feel like to change this belief?

She tapped the points:

I thought it was not OK for me to be happy...I have thought that my stepmother had power over me...my body is cowering...my body is afraid...my body is still connected to my stepmother's eyes. I am wondering what it would be like to disconnect from my stepmother's eyes...I wonder what it would feel like if I looked away... I wonder what it would feel like to look away from my stepmother.

We tapped for all the feelings connected to looking away from her stepmother's eyes, and for feeling like she was leaving people behind.

"I don't know a lot about the Chinese culture," I said, as we tapped, "but I know that these steps you are taking go against centuries of conditioning. Honor yourself for having the courage it takes to look away."

As we tapped through the points, I just talked about what was coming to mind for me as I felt into Christine's situation:

"As you think back into the culture and tradition of the position of women and how it is maintained, give some thought to the cost to a woman's own individual personality that was required of each woman. Note also what a good strategy it was for a nation of people to maintain harmony in inharmonious times. In some way that feels right to you, honor and acknowledge that those times that created this way of maintaining and creating harmony are over now. A new way of being is being asked for. The new way still contains the same honor and integrity, and offers the same harmony, but without that deep cost to individual women of giving up their individuality on behalf of the whole.

"Think of yourself as a woman who is being called to find a new way of being that allows you to have a sense of inner integrity, inner harmony, and power, in a way that women in your cultural past, for centuries, didn't know. Take a moment to acknowledge that those times are over now. Women had to be like that. But those times are no longer happening. You are free now to choose a new way of being in yourself that is just as honorable and creates a new and different kind of harmony. Ask your soul what would it feel like to feel this way."

Christine said with delight in her voice, "My soul is showing me a picture of a dancing joyous feeling. Free. The word 'fairies' comes to me. I am not worried. I feel this very small and deep inside my chest. Hmm. It is covered with a lot of 'but-but-but.'"

"Centuries of buts!" I put in. I felt that this session was for planting the seeds of a new belief that could grow, and maybe even dispel the buts in the process. In another session, we could deal individually with any remaining buts. "So Christine," I continued, "would you be willing to put that old belief—that 'it is not OK for me to be happy'— into your Museum of Old Beliefs? Would you be willing to make a little more space in your chest for something new? I am not asking you to change dramatically but to take a step in a healing direction."

She took another step forward and laid that old belief reverently, with honor, into what she imagined her Museum of Old Beliefs would look like.

We tapped here, too:

> *With honor and reverence, lay that old belief to rest. You are honoring and reverencing your culture, the deep, powerful, and profound beliefs, saying to yourself, "I want to bring with me the blessings of that culture, but leave behind what has been painful for me so that I can create something new that has even deeper and more profound honor that my soul will be proud to carry."*

Step in a Healing Direction

Now I had Christine step to the top of the circle, and feel joyous free dancing fairies, even if surrounded by buts. I asked her, "If you could put the 'free dancing fairies' feeling into words as a new belief about your happiness, what would you say?"

She replied, "I am at peace with my being happy. And I feel a hesitating inside. It's a different language! Part of me is going 'huh?' But yes, I can say it."

I wanted her to understand how deeply I sensed the effort and the effects of her taking this step. Though my life obviously hasn't been grounded in her culture, I have felt in myself what she was feeling.

What we do and feel and think changes the evolution of human consciousness (or perhaps it is the consciousness of evolution). When any of us frees a constricting belief, we are working on behalf of all of us. I believe that this is the spiritual purpose of our time—learning how to feel a part of a group and to stand fully in our presence as an individual at the same time.

Christine said, "I am crying, so some part of me understands."

I went on: " So stand now in this place of 'being at peace with being happy.'"

We tapped:

Especially because I am standing in this new place, of being open to being at peace with being happy for myself, I honor the centuries of tradition that brought me here.

Especially because I am taking this step that looked like it would be stepping away from all that I knew and loved, I acknowledge that I am stepping more deeply into a sense of reverence for harmony and knowing my own unique power.

I am taking this step, on behalf of myself and all Chinese women, I am choosing to be open to believing that it is OK for me to be happy.

Next Christine stepped into the Open to Believing Place, and we tapped:

Especially because I honor my Chinese heritage, I am choosing to honor it in a different way, by being open to harmony within myself.

Especially because I am acting on behalf of all Chinese women across space and time, and I am acting on behalf of myself as an individual, I am choosing to be open to believing that it really is OK for me to be happy, and I am feeling those dancing joyous free fairies in my heart!

We tapped for:

Dancing joyous free fairies in my heart...open to believing it is OK for me to be happy...I acknowledge all these buts...I acknowledge all the fears...I acknowledge all those different feelings, and still I am open to believing it's OK for me to be happy...And in some way I am thanking my stepmother, too, because she wasn't able to experience this, and how she acted toward me made it possible for me to be thinking the way I am thinking today ...I am open to dancing joyous free fairies deep inside my chest...I am opening to my own free spiri...I love this feeling...I deserve this.

I asked Christine to close her eyes and breathe deeply and easily. While she tapped on the side of her hand, I spoke, bringing back all her thoughts and images and weaving in some of my own as the spirit of the moment moved me:

"In your imagination, look back around the circle from where you stand now. Remember the place you started: 'It's not OK for me to be happy. Whenever I start feeling happy, the veil comes down. I see my stepmother's eyes. I chose to look away, because looking into her eyes was toxic for me.'

"You believed in and valued your own life strongly enough that you were willing to take some steps to save yourself, because you are worth saving. You looked away from your stepmother's eyes, all the fear and sadness in all those women's eyes, going back thousands of years, on behalf of what is right for you as an individual. On behalf of yourself and who you are and what is right for you, you put that old way of being and thinking into an old temple museum, full of old cultural beliefs that now longer serve you in the way they were meant to and would have hundreds of years ago.

"You took the guidance of your own soul, the guidance of your inner self, the guidance of your own body, and you stepped into a place of new belief. It feels like dancing joyous free spirits deep inside your chest. You did this even though you know that this is an unfamiliar path, not only for you, but also for millions of women who share your thoughts and feelings, but who may not yet have traveled quite as far along the path of thinking that you have. You are willing to incorporate the best of what is in the past and leave behind only what has been toxic for you.

"Now you are open to believing in the future of your own free spirit, and that it is OK for you to be happy. In fact it's quite a good thing for you to be happy! You recognize that there is more inner work to do with all of this, more honoring and reverencing and integrating, and you can do this in a way that will make you happy."

I left a moment of silence for these words to integrate.

After a bit, Christine shared these closing words: "I am filled right now with so much gratitude for your clarity and help. I can feel honored and safe. It feels like things have moved. My body feels very peaceful—great knowing seems to come to me, not in a burst of light but from a place of strength of knowing that I can do a better job now of bringing harmony. I shall take your words as a reminder for when I do forget."

Later, Christine sent me this e-mail:

> Dear Rue:
>
> After our session today, I just spent a quiet hour by myself, reflecting and reveling in the good feelings I held within me. I went outside to sit in my garden. I closed my eyes for a moment, enjoying the sun and feeling the gentle wind on my face. I heard the hummingbird calls and the songs of robins. The air was perfumed with the late blooms of roses.
>
> I decided to open my eyes, and invited my soul to see the world with me.

I noticed that sun feels warmer. There is joy reflected on the leaves as the sunrays bounced off it. The air smelled so sweet. I feel glad to be alive! My heart was filled with joy and I love it! I feel like jumping up and down like a kid for the sheer joy of loving the moment in my life.

Then I heard "It is from this place of abundance that you can truly give what you have."

I understand the wisdom that one can give only what one has. So being in a place of absolute joy is not a selfish endeavor but an important medicine in my life.

I truly am honored to have had this opportunity to work with you today!

With love and appreciation,

Christine

Seeing and Hearing Yourself

If you have felt invisible and unheard, now is a good time to learn to see and hear yourself. That is the root of the issue, of course: When there is no one around to mirror to us the goodness of who we really are, we don't learn how to see ourselves, or hear ourselves. EFT can help us do that, and also, perhaps, can help us begin the process of forgiving those people who raised us who couldn't see their own truth, and therefore couldn't see ours.

Make a list of the most difficult times when you felt unheard and unseen, and note the beliefs that you formed about yourself and your worth in the world as a result. Tap for all the aspects of each of these events, and for any throat, mouth, or jaw issues you may have, imagining them as symptoms of not being able to speak up for yourself.

Adopt the intention deep inside yourself that you will always seek to give yourself the benefit of the doubt, find the positive intention in all that you do, and intend to see and hear and feel the goodness in you. You deserve this.

Your family would have given this visibility and hearability to you if they could have, if someone had mirrored that capacity to them. Think of yourself as an ancestor: Offer your transforming life as a resource to those who will come after you in the tapestry of your family's ancestral story.

11

Stand Up for Yourself

For a sensitive person, and for anyone, really, healing stuffed emotions lies in learning how to stand up for oneself. Like speaking for oneself, this topic illustrates how useful metaphoric language is in working with a presenting issue. Think of all the ways we use the word "stand" to indicate how we are shaping ourselves in relation to our world: outstanding, standing out, understanding, stand for, stand in for, a standout player, upstanding, and many more. How we stand up for ourselves indicates how we feel about ourselves. It is worth exploring this metaphor when you have symptoms showing up in your legs, knees, or lower back, or when you have a hard time doing what feels intuitively right for you and are expected to do something quite different. Here are two examples of tapping sessions that helped each person stand up for herself in a new way.

Madelyn: From Weak in the Knees to Standing Up for Herself

One day, Madelyn (you met her in chapter 4) came in feeling "weak in the knees, a hurt, numb, buzzy feeling." When she was sitting down the sensation was a 3, but standing up, it was a 7. She said, "It feels like I want to collapse, you know, the feeling you get before you are about to faint." She is in management in a large company, and she talked about having gone the week before to a meeting on the East Coast.

Traveling had been a nightmare, with cancelled and rescheduled planes, missed connections, and people at the other end left hanging. In addition to the stress of the journey, she was feeling guilty and mad at herself, because she had turned responsibility for the trip over to her colleague, who she had seen as a seasoned traveler. But he wasn't as aware as he might have been, creating many difficulties that became overwhelming for her.

Madelyn started feeling dizzy and weak-kneed there in the airport, and those feelings increased over the challenging next few days of the scheduled meetings. She was able to stuff her usual feelings of frustration and inadequacy for the duration of the meetings, but she said, "I paid later." When she began talking about an upcoming meeting at which she feared she would be asked to take on a major national project, her discomfort in her knees went up to "at least an 8."

Madelyn was a very successful, high-achieving perfectionist, inclined to "push through" whatever she was feeling to get the job done right. She was also a highly sensitive introvert, if she were being who she really was, which she hadn't been. Not surprisingly, she had suffered from fibromyalgia for many years, and been diagnosed with breast cancer two years earlier. On her return from the business trip, she had gone to her physical therapist who does myofascial release for treatment of her knees; the PT said that her fascia is always tight in that area and, in fact, all over her body.

Ignoring my usual tendency to go deeper and deeper with my perpetual curiosity about the origin of these patterns, this time I just went to work right there with the knees, these "weak knees," "hurt, numb, buzzing knees," "wanting-to-collapse knees." Her intensity rating went down by one point.

Thinking about knees metaphorically, I asked Madelyn to say more about feeling weakness in her knees ("What is bringing you to your knees?") and she started talking about the upcoming meeting at which she was afraid they were going to ask her to take the lead on a major project, and she just didn't feel "up" to doing that. Not enough "down" time, she would "end 'up' in pain," "I'm not good at relating to all those 'up' sales guys," "I don't think well on my feet."

I was starting to notice a pattern here…

She went on, saying that she felt she didn't have any choice, she really should lead this project, she hadn't told anyone about the fibromyalgia (and wouldn't have told anyone about the cancer, was planning to get right back to work after surgery, but then was forced to tell people about the chemotherapy). "What will people think? They will think I am wimping out."

So here were some good phrases to use in the Setup and on the tapping points. Her intensity rating was down to a 5 by this time.

Thinking about the physiological and metaphorical role of knees, we began to talk about standing up for oneself and speaking up for oneself, how hard that was for her. "I'm not good at asking for what I need, asking to be heard. It feels like I am 'hollering into the night and no one is there,'" she said. "But I am finding that overachieving doesn't bring the same satisfaction that it used to."

I was wondering out loud how we could reframe and work with the idea of standing up for yourself. I was asking evocative questions like:

What actually holds you up?

How could you reframe using your knees for holding yourself up?

What do your knees want for you by wanting to fall down, and hurting when you aren't standing up for what is really true for you?

We fell into one of those serendipitous conversational flows that seem to come when you open yourself to your intuition and wonder out loud and internally about something, and I got a great insight into and learning about fibromyalgia.

All of her life Madelyn had been forcing herself to do things she didn't feel comfortable with, and had developed a kind of rigid forcing tension throughout her body that became very painful. The pain came from chronically tense muscles, held in a protective, defensive readiness, which had led to contracted, tight, stiff fascia all over her body, creating constant pain.

Fascia is the tough, connective tissue web between the skin and the body's underlying structure of muscle and bone. (It is what you see if you skin a raw chicken, that almost transparent sheet between the skin and the muscle.) It surrounds every organ, duct, nerve, blood vessel, muscle, and bone of the pelvic cavity. Fascia has a tensile strength of more than two thousand pounds per square inch. It can become severely bound by shock, trauma, and stress. Unresolved emotional pain and trauma turns to physical tightness in the body. As the fascia tightens, the body must work harder and harder just to perform daily activities, leading to fatigue and feeling very like depression.

Medical intuitive Caroline Myss has said that "our biography becomes our biology." Neuroscientist Bessel van der Kolk says, "The body keeps the score." It occurred to me that the fascia is one of the scoreboards for the body.

Together, tapping and talking, Madelyn and I created an image of the fascia as having become a painful suit of armor that was trying to hold her up, with all of the limiting beliefs that she carried about who she must be in the world to succeed—the shoulds, the have-tos, the "I have no choice," "What will they think of me if I don't?"—all the pushing toward perfection and performance.

The fascia is meant to support, not hold us up. Tap tap tap…

This painful suit of armor…trying to help me stand up for myself…trying to protect me from being hurt, ignored, rejected…holding my Self tightly to keep it saf…this painful suit of armor in my knees.

As we continued to tap through the points, sometimes pausing on one point to talk and tap, I asked Madelyn what would work better as a support for holding her up, and where she would feel that in her body.

"It would be a feeling that I can just freely connect with others," she said, "and open to a flow of love and affection, letting that flow out to others and feeling it flow back into me, no longer feeling separate from them." She felt this in her chest, as movement and flow going out and returning.

Tapping on the Karate Chop point, we walked through feeling a free-flowing connection with people she loved, and then moved into experiencing the flow with others who were more challenging, even those "up" salesmen.

Suddenly she said, "When I go to that meeting, I really can't take the lead in that national project that they were trying to get me to take on. I'm really not up to it. But using the cancer experience as an excuse feels like I am trying to worm my way out of something."

I asked her to find a way to frame it positively, and she flowed right into this wonderful, clear strong statement:

"I will say to them that I have had a lot of life experience, including being sick, and that has taught me what is really important in life, and what I can and can't do, and what I want and don't want to do, and I *don't* want to do this."

Standing up for herself. Her knees felt fine!

Martha: "I Couldn't Stand Those Crowds!"

In a recent class on EFT and intuition, I asked everyone to think of a decision they had to make, one that they were feeling conflict over and found themselves over-thinking. The volunteer this time was Martha, who had an interesting dilemma. It wasn't earth-shaking as decisions go, but the inner conflict pointed to some deep beliefs and an inner story that was hanging up her deliberations.

Martha had been invited by friends to go hear the Dalai Lama speak. She really wanted to go, and yet she knew that there would be a huge crowd of people there. "I have difficulty with a large crowd," she said. "Should I go and just force myself to deal with crowds? Or not go? Would that be wimping out? Maybe I should just tough it out and soldier on."

I asked Martha to imagine going to the talk. What happened in her body when she thought about it?

"There is an 'Oh no!' feeling, a tightening in my chest, a bracing and a pushing-away feeling in my heels. I couldn't stand those crowds!" (It turned out that she had chronic pain in her feet—interesting that her symptoms showed up there!) The emotion felt like fear, and the intensity was a 9 out of 10. So the initial fear and body response was an intuitive no in Martha's body.

In this particular session, I didn't want just to help Martha eliminate her fear on the spot with EFT. My intention was to help her set herself on a course of paying attention to, noticing, and honoring what was right for her in the moment. In another session, it might be appropriate to deal directly with the fear, and its roots. In psychology, this fear is called social anxiety disorder. That term is, in itself, an implied criticism, however, and feeds directly into our suspicion that "there is something wrong with me." (The odd dichotomy of a healing profession reinforcing a person's negative belief system—it happens more than we realize—is a subject that I want to explore another time.) Here in this work with Martha, it felt to me that this honoring piece should come first for her. We think with our bodies. EFT can help you come home to find out what your body is thinking.

"So, Martha," I said, "your body is saying no. This is your first intuitive response. As we tap, notice whether that no becomes clearer as a no, or if it is transforming to something else. We will also want to deal with your second-guessing yourself by saying, 'Maybe I'm wimping out, I should soldier on, I should tough it out.' Those are the kinds of beliefs that directly interfere with our inner knowing about what is right for us."

We tapped:

Even though I have this strong reaction when I think about going to see the Dalai Lama because I really don't like crowds, I accept myself anyway, I accept how I feel, and I appreciate that my body is giving me this information.

Right away, Martha could feel resistance in herself to accepting that she felt this way.

Even though I don't accept this reaction in myself ... it sets up a dissonance inside ... I don't really even know what I think, I can't get any guidance about what I'm supposed to do—I wish the Dalai Lama would just tell me what to do! ... I accept myself anyway, even if I don't, and I am curious to find out if I can think more deeply about this.

Tapping the points:

I don't accept that I am having this reaction.

It makes me think I'm wimpy.

I'm wimping out.

I really ought to soldier on and tough it out.

I should be able to do this!

What is wrong with me?

And anyway I want to see the Dalai Lama.

I am having this conflict inside.

I want to go see the Dalai Lama.

But I can't do those crowds.

This conflict is blocking my inner knowing.

As a test of our work so far, I asked Martha to think of being in the crowd now, and notice what happens inside.

"I don't feel quite so fearful, but I'm still not too enthusiastic," she said doubtfully.

"Right now we are not trying to get rid of the fear to make it possible for you to go see the Dalai Lama," I offered. "We are just honoring your body's intuitive responses, sensing into what your inner self really prefers that you do. There are no right answers here, no expectations."

The image came up in Martha's mind of going hiking instead. I asked her to get a sense of what happens inside when she imagined going hiking. It was an opening, expansive feeling. Interestingly, the fear had gone down to a 4, but the resistance to being in the large crowds was still strong, a 7 or 8.

> *Even though I still have some fear, and I accept that I have it, even though I might think I am wimpy, I am curious to learn the deeper wisdom of my body for an answer in this situation.*

> *Even though I still have some fear, and a strong sense of resistance, I accept that these are my inner responses, and I am wondering what this means. I am open to my body telling me more.*

> *Even though I have worried that I was wimping out by saying no, and I thought I should say yes just to soldier on and tough it out, I accept that my body is giving me a message, and I am wanting to deepen into my own truth here. What is right for me?*

Tapping the points:

> *I couldn't do those crowds.*

But maybe I should make myself do it anyway.

I'd kind of like to go hiking instead—that feels like a yes.

Crowds are overwhelming to me.

I had been experiencing the fear.

This sense of bracing in my feet.

This sense of tightening in my abdomen.

I'm wondering what to do.

What is right for me?

Do I want to go see the Dalai Lama?

Would I rather go hiking?

What do I really want?

What would I get from seeing the Dalai Lama?

What would I get from going hiking?

Interesting that my feet are my resistance meter—and here I am thinking about going hiking—that's where my feet want to go!

I'm asking for guidance.

I am asking for my own deeper wisdom in this situation.

I asked Martha, "What is coming into your mind as we tap?"

Martha responded, "There is sadness, that it looks like I don't want to go to the talk. It would be a unique experience, I would be with my friends, I might never have this experience again, the loss of a unique opportunity, it makes me sad to think I am not going."

I suggested this: "Feel into your sadness, consider it, and ask inside 'Is there another part of me that would be willing to go and deal with the crowds? Is there a way that I could do this and keep myself feeling OK about the crowds?'"

Martha answered (we were continuously tapping through the points as we were speaking), "Whenever I think about the crowds, I get a breathless fear. The answer I get is no."

"Just remember, I am not trying to force you into going," I said. "We are inviting the deeper awareness in you to come up with a solution that makes you feel OK—good, even—about whatever you decide."

We continued tapping:

Even though I am still feeling breathless and fearful about braving the crowds, and at the same time I am feeling sad about not going, I accept that I have all these responses in me, and I want to feel good about the decision that I make.

Even though I have fear and sadness bot…and part of me really wants to go see the Dalai Lama…and still part of me really doesn't want to deal with the crowds, I accept that there is this confusion and conflict inside, and I am seeking a deeper resolution.

We tapped through the points, naming these conflicts.

Afterward, when we again tested her response to going to the event and it still came up not very enthusiastic, I asked Martha, as she tapped on the side of her hand to consider this important question: "How can I make this situation work for me?" I said, "Think about how you might not go see the Dalai Lama. And, on the other hand, there are reasons why you want to go. This is a rare occasion, you would be in the presence of a rare being, the purpose of going is to get a sense of his wisdom and of understanding his presence in the world. Are there other ways to do that besides challenging yourself to do something you feel uncomfortable doing? Is there another way that could be better for you, right now—videos, DVDs, books, speaking afterward with your friends who are going? Again, I am not trying to influence your thinking, just offering other possibilities."

And then I asked, "How does it feel to honor your body's resistance and find other ways of gaining what you want from the event?"

Martha said, "My resistance is still strong, but it is not fear now. It feels like deeper wisdom for myself. I feel it is really not the right thing for me to go."

We tested her earlier belief: "If I don't go, I will be wimping out." How true did that feel now?

Martha said, "It doesn't feel true any more at all. I know now that if I did go, I wouldn't be listening to my inner voice, my own truth for right now."

We did a final round of tapping:

I am choosing to honor myself and find alternative ways to accomplish what I want, while at the same time honoring what I need.

It is not the right thing for me to be in this large crowd.

I honor my body's wisdom for making that clear to me.

I can take a stand on my own behalf, and find different ways to achieve the same end.

I understand I'm not wimping out, in fact, I am taking a stand on my own behalf. This is a very brave act on the part of my feet! Standing up for myself!

I honor myself for making this choice.

I choose to find other ways to honor my intention of encountering what the Dalai Lama offers, ways that are more appropriate for me right now.

Some time in the future I may choose to deal with the fear.

It is up to me.

This is my intuition, and I'm sticking to it!

Standing Up for You

When you find yourself wanting to stand up for yourself in stronger, more effective ways, you have the tool of EFT at your fingertips. Begin by thinking of specific incidents where you felt a conflict around taking some step or action. A part of you wants to take the step or action, but another part of you is holding back. Or you feel a strong resistance to doing something that "everyone else" is doing or thinks you should do, and at the same time you want to please those people and you think you are a wimp for not just going for it. Make a list of times like this in your life, making sure you include incidents from your childhood.

Tap for each incident, for all the feelings you had, for all the beliefs about yourself that came up, for how your body felt then or feels now when you think of the incident, for any symptoms that seem related to the issue of standing up for yourself.

Use tapping phrases like:

Even though I'm not good at asking for what I need, or asking to be heard, I am choosing to honor myself and find alternative ways to accomplish what I want, while at the same time honoring what I need.

Even though it is not the right thing for me to _____, I honor my body's wisdom for making that clear to me.

Even though I don't think well on my feet, I can take a stand on my own behalf, and find different ways to achieve the same end.

Even though I really want their approval, I understand I'm not wimping out, in fact, I am taking a stand on my own behalf. This is a very brave act on the part of my feet/legs/back/knees! I am standing up for myself!

Even though I want their approval, I honor my need for connection, and connecting with myself is the most important act I can take.

Even though I feel all this fear, I choose to find other ways to honor my intentions that are more appropriate for me right now. Sometime in the future, I may choose to deal with the fear. It is up to me.

As sensitive people, our tendency is always to try to "measure up" to someone else's standard of what is right for us, because we grew up being asked, "What's wrong with you that you can't do this?" We can use EFT to learn what is truly right for us, and support ourselves in our decisions, no matter what "everyone else" thinks.

12

Canary in the Coal Mine—
Healing Yourself Is Healing the World

When I first thought to ask questions of the world as if it were an oracle, I asked this question: "What makes people frame their experience negatively?" I was thinking that if I could come to understand the deep cause of this seemingly inevitable process, I could gain a glimpse into how healing happens. The World as Oracle is a way of getting guidance, actually asking the world to speak an answer to your question in the form of what you notice in a given period of time. So I spoke to the Universe, stating that for the next twenty minutes I would hold this question about framing our sensitivity negatively while I paid close attention to what caught my awareness, trusting that I would be offered an answer as I drove home in my car.

Right away on the drive, I saw a billboard that read "Overworking your heart?" Then I saw a bumper sticker that read, "If you praise your kids they will bloom" (the reverse implication being, of course, that if you don't praise your kids, they will wilt). And then I went by a movie theater with a double feature that ran two titles together looking like one: "Imaginary Heroes Born in a Brothel."

I thought about all of these messages together as an answer to my question. Doesn't that run-together movie title sound like us: highly sensitive, bold, bright, beautiful sovereign beings, come from the imaginal realm to be the shining heroes of our own story and that of the planet, born into a bewildering environment of distorted concepts of love, power, and purpose?

Doing our best, battling our inner demons with faith and courage, overworking our hearts, believing that we are not up to the desperate task of protecting our spirit in an unsafe, unfriendly universe. And never having gotten enough praise ourselves, from parents who never got enough praise, because our grandparents never got enough praise, we wilt.

On the whole, humanity doesn't know yet that the very universe blooms when any of us smiles.

I believe that each of us is called to the earth, by the earth itself, to offer the blessing of our personal transformation. I have heard so many sensitive people lament that their lives have been wasted, trying in vain to deal with all the pain. What we pick up in our sensitivity is there for all, if they were but sensitive enough to notice it. We are the canaries in the coal mine, unable to ignore the pain within and around us. What is truly asked of us is our day-to-day living into healing. It is not that we "get healed" and then go out into the world to "save it" or do "good works." In healing the wounds of our beliefs about our sensitivity,

I believe that we heal our spirit. With every person that does this, the world is healed a little more.

Here is a tapping script that can help you reframe how you think of your sensitivity and its value in the world.

A Tapping Script for Turning in a Healing Direction

We can stop obsessively tracking our failures. The engine that runs all this is our intention. We can turn ourselves in a healing direction. We can start paying attention to what we need in this very moment. We can be directed by our positive intention. We can change how we feel about being "too sensitive," and we can celebrate who we are. The world needs what we know!

Even though I am used to tracking my failures, and the people I learned how to do this from were really good at it, I love and accept myself anyway.

Even though my family story is all about trying to prevent failures, I accept myself and I accept my family. We are all doing the best we can.

Even though I have to be perfect so that I don't fail, I accept myself, and I forgive myself for putting all this pressure on myself. I just haven't known any other way!

Even though failure is not allowed in my family, I accept myself and how I feel. I honor myself for how hard this has been for me.

Even though I can't speak up for myself...

Even though I fear that if I am noticed I will be judged....

Even though I worry what's wrong with me...

Especially because I deserve to, I am ready to dissolve this old approach to telling the story of my life. I intend to do this, starting in this moment!

Now let's repeat the tapping list that framed all the problems we experience from our sensitivity, and reframe them again as our gifts. Then we can make them even better!

Again, the following words are mine. Change them however you like to find phrases that fit you and feel good to you. Maybe you like to speak in superlatives—use those. Maybe you have more profound or more spiritual ways of expressing what is truly the best, loveliest, and greatest about you—go for it! Use your best words, ones that make you light up inside!

Tap using the normal EFT spots. But instead of saying "Even though..." try saying "Especially because... " Take out the old phrases in the parentheses and replace them in each case with what follows:

Especially because (I worry that I am too sensitive) I love that I am so sensitive, I choose to deepen and expand my sensitivity in powerful wonderful ways.

Especially because (I feel so deeply) I have this fabulous capacity to feel deeply, I choose to accept it as an honor, and learn how to share what I know in ways that are helpful.

Especially because (I think my sensitivity is a weakness) I like that I am sensitive, I choose to love, appreciate, and honor this powerful, world-changing soul quality that I have been so blessed with. The world needs what I have to offer! I am ready to be more!

Especially because (I think something is wrong with me, that it is my fault) I believe that I am a good person, I choose to open to what I know in my deepest heart that I can become! I love and appreciate and honor this precious being that I am!

Especially because (I wish things didn't bother me so much) I am glad that I am so aware, I choose to trust the Universe to handle the problems and I use my awareness and my energy to make a difference in this world that I care so much about.

Continue tapping beginning with the phrase "Especially because" (EB):

EB I have this wonderful gift of being able to think and speak in abstract big-picture, profound concepts, I choose to deepen and strengthen my ability to be an "imagineer," and I use my manifestation ability even better so that the goodness I sense has a space to live in, in this world.

EB being cooperative and diplomatic is important to me, I choose to break the rules that aren't working for me and make new ones that feel right, in ways that still honor other people's integrity and intentions.

EB I hunger for deep and meaningful relationships, I make creating and maintaining a good and satisfying relationship with myself my first priority.

EB I value personal growth, authenticity, and integrity, I choose to discover my own strengths and excellence, and do everything I can to enlarge them.

EB I am internally deeply caring, I choose to take just as good care of myself as I do of _____.

EB I am deeply committed to the positive and the good, I choose to honor that commitment to myself!

EB I have a mission to bring peace to the world, I choose a mission of bringing peace into my own life.

EB I have a strong personal morality, I choose to stand even taller in my own strong life!

EB I often make extraordinary sacrifices for someone/something I believe in, I choose myself!

EB I think I am unusual and unique, I choose to stand up for myself and express who I am with love and a light heart. No one can resist that.

EB I have a good imagination, I choose to find amazing ways of bringing magic into my life where there was only misery before. Evolution itself depends on how good I get at this. The world needs what I have to offer!

What a blessing we have in EFT. In the use of this blessing for ourselves and others, we can touch the space in each of us where we become a blessing, just by being. No expectations to meet, nothing we have to do to become worthy. I believe that it is our healing process itself that is the blessing. All we have to do is intend it. When we live the questions, as the German poet Rilke said, rather than struggle to find answers, we find ourselves living into the answers. And there, in that flow, lies the healing. Nothing is wasted. Every one of our moments counts.

Celebrate your sensitivity with EFT!

13

EFT Eight-Week Program for HST—
From "What's Wrong with Me?" to Celebrating Sensitivity

Week One: Break Out of the Cage of the PASST (Pain, Anger, Sadness, Stress, Trauma)

On the left side of a piece of paper, make a list of everything you don't like about being sensitive. Include comments people have made to you, both in your childhood and more recently, and your own critical self-talk.

On the right side of the paper, list every single good quality that you can think of in yourself, including what your parents, teachers, friends, guardian angels, God, and pets (if they could talk) have said or would say about you that is good.

Create tapping routines that begin with the statements from the left column. Add "I deeply and completely love and accept myself, and _____." Fill in the blank with one of the comments from the right column.

Example:

> *Even though I am so easily hurt and upset, I deeply and completely love and accept myself, and I appreciate that I have this wonderful capacity to feel so deeply.*

Breaking Out of the Cage of the PASST

Begin by asking yourself:

1. What have people said to me about my sensitivity?

    Tap on: *Even though people (my mother/father/friend/boss) have said _____, I deeply and completely love and accept myself anyway.*

2. How has that made me feel? Where do I feel these feelings in my body?

    Tap on the feelings and emotion held in your body.

3. What did I come to believe about myself as a result?

    Tap to transform the beliefs to ones that serve you better.

4. Choose a specific disturbing incident from your life connected with being sensitive.

    Make a movie or inner story of the specific incident. Give it a title. Note details: clear, fuzzy, movement, still, sound, silent, and so on.

    Tap on the title: *Even though I have this _____ (title) story in my body about being sensitive, I deeply and completely love and accept myself.*

    Tap while you watch and feel the story unfold.

    Tap on the worst parts.

Tap on all the aspects.

Note what has changed in your response to the story after you tap. Check your 0–10 level of intensity. Repeat the process until your intensity is down to 0, or until you feel much better about the specific incident.

Read chapter 3and follow the many tapping suggestions and routines there.

Practice catching yourself in self-criticism, reformulate the thought with EFT to one that feels better, and find ways to honor your sensitivity this week!

Week Two: Heal Your Broken Heart

Think of as many incidents as you can that have been painful for you, remembering that as a sensitive person you have been impacted more deeply than most people by a look, a word, a tone of voice, a gesture.

Using the following Story Map as a guide, tap through each of these incidents until you think of each one in a different way. Find a way to tell a story about each incident that makes you feel better, not worse.

Story Map

I had to _____or else _____.

A belief (behavior/outlook on life/self-image) about this that I got from my family is _____.

That has created a problem in my life because (or when) _____.

A good example of that was the time when _____ [particular, specific].

The worst part of that particular incident was _____.

That made me feel _____.

It made me think I was _____.

I feel that in my body here: _____ [name part].

Sometimes I even think maybe I don't deserve _____.

But deep inside, I yearn for _____.

If I had that, I would feel _____.

So now I forgive myself. I was doing the best I could. I choose to _____ instead.

This Story Map is simple, though not always easy to fill out. Just coming up with the answers may be a triggering experience. Tap for any emotions that come up for you as you fill in the sentences.

Next, you might take each of the completed sentences, make a Setup statement from it, and tap through the story this way, until no part of the story is still a trigger. It is also possible to use these sentences more fluidly in the EFT session, adding them as phrases in the tapping process as the need arises.

Read chapter 4 for descriptions of other people's experiences.

This week, practice changing your story about what you have experienced into one that feels better to you!

Week Three:
Change Your Beliefs and Keep the Change

Come back to the list of good things about yourself that you have been adding to over the last two or three weeks. (You have been adding to it, haven't you? If not, start now!)

Read chapters 8 and 9 to get some ideas about the beliefs in your family that have been handed down through the generations.

How might these beliefs impact a sensitive person? The real question to ask here is: How might these beliefs have evolved to protect a sensitive temperament (and then over time become ingrained and unconscious as "right" or the "way it is")?

Make a list of the main beliefs. If it helps, write a paragraph or a page about your family, letting your thoughts flow in no particular order about what they seem to believe.

Go back and separate out the sentences and phrases that sound like your family's "culture of beliefs."

Using ideas from both of these lists, make up some tapping routines for yourself. Here are some examples:

Even though all my negative thinking about myself became physical neglect, and that probably contributed to the symptoms I have now and who knows what else, I accept myself anyway, and I choose to believe that I can put my attention on what is good about me instead. Maybe that will help my well-being! Hmm...

Even though my body has been in pain, I am wondering now if there is a connection with all the painful beliefs and thoughts that I have been feeding it. I know that there are lots of good qualities about me, and I wholeheartedly believe that there is a possibility to change my self-harming habits.

Even though I have had a habit of thinking negatively about myself, I can see that maybe that is hurting me, and maybe my body had to get sick to get my attention. I honor myself for being strong and a survivor, and I can use my ability to learn, seek, and find out how things work to change my thought habits. What if I can help my body to work better this way?

Tapping on the points:

I have been hard on myself.

I am pretty self-critical.

I have had some bad thinking habits that were turning into physical neglect.

I accept that I have been doing that.

Maybe it contributed to my illnesses.

But that is the way I learned to think in my family.

Everyone thought that way.

I thought they were right.

What if they were wrong?

What if they just never had anyone to help them to recognize bad thinking habits?

What if they thought those thoughts were the truth?

I love that I have a good imagination.

I could imagine something different for myself.

I want to be fairer to myself.

I want justice for myself!

I know that I can be creative with words. I want to find some better ones to use on my behalf.

I am smart and intuitive.

I am a good teacher.

I can teach myself some new habits here!

What a smart thing to do!

Even though this persistent putting myself down has probably led to undervaluing myself (even though being so self-critical has led me to undervalue myself), I accept that I have been doing that and I take responsibility for it.

Even though being so self-critical has shaped me, and created the life I am living now, including any illness and pain, I wonder if I could take a different shape? I know I have lots of good qualities to shape my identity around.

Even though the shape I have taken has been creating a destiny that doesn't feel so good to me, and I must have thought a person's destiny was set in stone, I choose to believe that there is a possibility for me to change my destiny for my real highest purpose in life. I know I can be more. The Universe will fit itself around the shape I choose to create.

Tapping on the points:

I have been devaluing myself.

I have been neglecting myself—physically, emotionally, spiritually—and I see that now.

I developed some bad thinking habits, and they shaped my values, my choices, and even my self-value.

I neglected myself.

I like making connections and I can now understand what I was doing.

That self-criticism was just my thoughts! It isn't the truth about me!

I really am a smart, intuitive, strong person.

I am honest. Honestly, I deserve better treatment from myself!

I am going to be more honest about my good qualities.

Hey, honesty is the best policy!

I have always wanted to know my purpose in life.

Maybe I have some clues here—what if my purpose is to change the way I think about myself? That would change everything!

By changing my thoughts, I could change my health.

By changing my thoughts, I could change my destiny!

What if Gandhi was right?

If my destiny is not turning out the way I want it to be, I can change my thoughts and change my destiny! It is up to me!

I like how that thought feels.

I deeply and completely accept this possibility for positive change.

I have always been creative. I can create a new destiny for myself!

I have a good imagination.

I can imagine myself right into my highest purpose in life.

Changing my thoughts about myself is my highest purpose.

Practice catching yourself in limiting beliefs this week. Ask yourself: *Is this really true? Do I have evidence that it is true? If it is not really true, what do I want to believe instead?*

Week Four: Change Your Responses (Emotional, Physical, Behavioral)

Ask yourself the questions listed here and any others that occur to you. While you do, listen inside. Pay attention to thoughts, worries, images, physical sensations, and feelings that arise. You can tap for your answers (see the examples). The phrases below in italics are one person's answers to these questions. Her issue was pain in her legs. Modify this protocol to fit your own needs. Your body is expressing the feelings that you couldn't. Teach yourself to care about what you feel.

Where, specifically, do you experience the pain?

Tops of my thighs, knees.

(Even though I have pain in…)

What is the worst part?

My knees are weak, I can't trust them.

(Even though my knees are weak…Even though I feel like I can't trust my knees…)

How would you describe it?

Soreness.

(Even though I have soreness in…)

Like what?

Like an ache. Knees ache.

(Even though my knees ache…)

Like my muscles are not toned.

(Even though it feels like my muscles are not toned…)

Continue to use each phrase in italics, sometimes as a Setup statement (Even though…) and sometimes as phrases to say while tapping on each point. Note: there is no way to do this wrong! You can't do any harm, only good.

When do you feel it? What triggers it?

When I am stressed and worried.

When did it start?

Exhausted from exercise.

Tension in my body.

When was the first time you felt something like this pain?

Sometime after that auto accident ten years ago.

(Work with all the aspects of the incident.)

Make a metaphor—what do your legs (your body part affected) feel like?

As if they are waking up from hibernation.

Like they haven't been used, no strength in them, like a bear coming out in spring.

I wove some imagery in later in the process: Bears are powerful...feels so good to come out of that cave... the fierce protectiveness and will to survive and thrive of the mother bear for her cubs/you for your own body.

How do you feel about your legs (body part) hurting?

It's embarrassing.

What, specifically, is embarrassing?

I feel out of shape.

Walking that short distance should not be an issue.

Frustrated with my body.

Mad at my body.

Note: "What, specifically...?" is an excellent question to ask to get deeper into vague answers. In EFT, the more specific you can get, the better it works.

If there were a deeper emotion under the pain, what would it be?

Worry that if I don't overcome this, pain in activity will get progressively worse.

Worry that the cycle of pain will get worse every time.

Worried what the future will be.

Anger—it's not fair!

What will that be like?

My physical abilities will be further limited.

Physically, I am not as strong as I want to be.

I think of myself as strong, but my body is keeping me back from being that.

When you worry, how do you do that?

A vicious mental circle: worry — exercise — pain — worry — stop exercise — worry…a gerbil wheel of worry.

We checked the intensity of her pain at this point and the pain was almost gone.

Here are some questions to ask to find positive things to add after you say, "Even though I have some remaining pain in my legs, I deeply and completely love and accept myself, and_____."

What do you want instead?

I want to fix my body, not mask the pain with drugs like my friend does.

I want a strong and healthy body.

What state of being would you have to be in for this to be true?

Excited about physical activity.

Peace, health, and well-being.

Knowing that I am enabling my body to feel good for my future.

If you were no longer worrying, what would you do instead?

Have new adventures, appreciate my body.

I choose:

To appreciate my health, my body.

(Even though I only have a little pain left in my legs, I choose…")

What specifically do you want to appreciate about your health and your body?

I choose to appreciate:

My legs — that I can still walk.

My legs for holding me up all these years.

My legs for helping me to stand up for myself.

My arms, that they can give people hugs.

My body, that it can feel joy.

I choose:

To look forward to each new adventure.

To look forward to the future.

To put my attention toward what I want, not what I fear.

Use your imagination, your curiosity, your associative thinking, and especially your humor to come up with images and phrases about the use and purpose, even the spiritual purpose, of the body part at issue for you, in this example, "legs." Of course you can do this with any subject, and this is what makes EFT so fun, I think. Be as wild and dramatic in your imagination as you can. Let healing be joyful!

For example, legs support you, they are your greatest friends, legs allow you to stand tall, to stand up for yourself, to take a stand, to stand out, to take you places, to get you where you want to go, to take you away from what you want to avoid, to jump for joy, to run away, to run to what you want, to kick things out of the way, to kick a path open for you, to be flexible, to be as short as you want or as tall as you are—inside and out.

You can sprinkle these phrases in as you tap.

Use your own imagination, let it run free!

Give your intuition its own legs!

Practice paying attention to and honoring the messages of your body this week. Practice caring about what you feel.

Read chapters 7 and 9 for more tapping ideas about tapping for physical and emotional feelings.

Week Five: Find the Positive
Intention of Feelings and Behaviors

Complete these sentences:

- People judge me because _____.
- Everyone loves it when I _____.
- When I do well, people feel _____.
- Nobody will let me _____.
- Everybody always tells me to _____.
- People just can't accept the fact that I _____.
- When I fail, everyone thinks _____.
- Nobody cares when I _____.
- Society keeps telling me I have to _____.
- Everyone expects me to _____.

The completed sentences make great EFT Setup statements. Just add "Even though..." and tap, recognizing that for a sensitive person, connection is all important. As children, we assume that the only way we can feel connected and feel like we belong is to do what we are told to do and be who we are told to be. We think that if we get approval, we are getting love and therefore must be lovable.

Make a list of the people whose approval you need, and for whom you tend to give yourself away. EFT can help you detach your need from people who continue to be unresponsive and only hurt and disappoint you when you try to get your needs for connection met with them.

Experiment with this tapping routine this week:

Take a moment to see if you are needing another person to act a certain way or if you are needing a situation to be a certain way. Feel that urge to control the person or the situation. Sometimes this need to control is driven by feeling threatened or insecure, so we'll address all these things as we tap.

Even though I have this need for people or things to be a certain way, I deeply accept myself.

And even though I feel this urge to control this person (or this situation), the truth is I can't control another person (or fully control any situation).

And even though I have this urge to control things, I'm willing to control what belongs to me and trust the process for the rest, and I'm choosing to feel more secure within myself no matter what happens. My security does not depend on the externals — it's an inside job.

Now tap with an alternating method, alternating the problem with positive truths:

>*What I need from the person or the situation.*
>
>*But no one can control it all.*
>
>*What I've wanted and needed from them.*
>
>*But no one can control it all.*
>
>*This urge to control people and situations.*
>
>*But I'll control what belongs to me and trust the process for the rest.*
>
>*Feeling insecure, needing to control things.*
>
>*I'll control what I can and trust the process.*
>
>*I'm choosing to feel more secure within myself no matter what happens.*
>
>*My security does not depend on the externals—it's an inside job.*

Take a deep breath. You might consider that the place where we have the most control in our lives is in our internal process. Our feelings and our thoughts are ours to work with. If we seek to control what is outside us, we'll continue to feel powerless, insecure, and stressed. But when we pay attention to our own feelings and internal reactions, we cultivate true power and true security—and EFT can really help us achieve that.

>*Even though I need this connection (use your words), I deeply accept myself…Even though I need their approval or I need them to like me (use your words), I deeply accept myself and I honor myself for my need for connection. Even though I feel this need, I'm willing to*

accept that I can't make this happen, and if that person is not available, I'm detaching now, choosing to connect with myself, to like myself, to approve of myself, and my connection with myself matters the most.

Tapping through the points (use your words):

What I need from them.

Maybe needing their approval.

Maybe needing them to like me.

It hurts that they won't give me that.

But I can't make it happen.

I honor my need for connection.

But I accept that I can't make it happen.

And I'm detaching from them now, detaching now, and I'm connecting with myself, liking myself, approving of myself—that's what matters.

(Adapted from a tapping routine crafted by Betty Moore-Hafter)

Read chapter 11 for help with standing up for your Self.

Practice disconnecting from toxic people and situations, and practice connecting with yourself this week!

Week Six: Learn What Is True for You— Use Your Intuition

It is easy to know what everyone wants of us. We have heard that all our lives. But how are we supposed to know what we want? What should we say with EFT after the "love and accept myself" part, if we can manage to say even that? Sensitive people have difficulty knowing "where they end and someone else begins." So many sensitive people grew up having to deny their own inner truth in order to support someone else's.

Read chapter 10 for some ideas about how to find and stand up for your own truth.

We have the best possible guide to what is best for us right here in our own bodies. Our bodies are intuition, personified—a simple but profound statement.

Start with this thought: Everything in life pretty much comes down to Yum and Yuck. We just need to learn how to know which is which.

This week, practice this exercise: Find Yum and Yuck in Your Body.

Begin by sitting quietly for just a moment, with your eyes closed.

Notice what happens inside when you say, "The world is an unfriendly place." Pay attention to thoughts and images that come up, and especially pay attention to how your body feels. Do you get tense? Where specifically in your body do you feel this question? What happens to your breathing?

Think of some of the experiences that irritate you or leave a "bad taste" in your mouth. (Don't do major traumas here, just small irritating events.) Again, notice where and how you experience these very different states of being in your body.

Say the word "no" and feel it inside. Notice where and how you experience this word in your body.

Now shift your position (when you change your position, you change your mind, and vice versa) and take some deep breaths.

Say inside, "The world is a friendly place." Again, notice thoughts and images, and especially notice, very specifically, what happens in your body. Where do you feel this statement? What happens to your breathing?

Think of some of your very favorite or peak experiences. They can be big or little, it doesn't matter. What counts is noticing how you felt at the time, in your body.

Say the word "yes" and feel it inside. Notice where and how you experience this word in your body.

Take a moment to gather all the impressions that your body has given you.

Sort them into Yum and Yuck.

Now you have a fail-safe way to make choices about what is right for you, from the inside out. Any time you have a choice to make, hold it in your awareness, and notice whether you get a Yum or a Yuck response from your body.

Here's an important point. The only way many people have known how to say yes to themselves is by saying no to what was in their environment. So when they first try this exercise, the feeling for yes is actually the feeling for no. This can be very confusing. Pay close attention to your inner experience when you do this exercise. Make sure you recognize this reversal, and get a bona fide yes in your body.

You, especially, deserve Yum!

Practice following your own truth this week!

Week Seven: Evidence of the Goodness in You

In 1957 in Bangkok, a group of monks from a monastery had to relocate their massive, ten-and-a-half-foot tall, 2.5-ton clay Buddha from their temple to a new location to make way for a new highway being built through the city. They used a crane to lift the statue, but it began to crack, and then rain began to fall. The head monk was concerned about damage to the sacred Buddha, and he decided to lower the statue down to the ground and cover it with a large canvas tarp to protect it from the rain.

Later that evening, the monk went to check on the Buddha. He shined a flashlight under the tarp, and noticed a gleam reflected through a crack in the clay. Wondering about what he saw, he got a chisel and hammer, and began to chip away at the clay. The gleam turned out to be gold, and many hours later the monk found himself face to face with an extraordinary, huge solid-gold Buddha.

Historians believe that several hundred years before this, the Burmese army was about to invade Thailand, then called Siam. The monks covered their precious statue with an eight-inch layer of clay to disguise its value. Very likely, the Burmese slaughtered all the Siamese monks, and the secret of the statue's golden essence remained intact until that day in 1957.

We are all like the golden Buddha in some way. We are covered with a protective layer, often so well covered that we have forgotten our true value.

Ask yourself the question: What was a time when I asked the Universe for help and the response came in an unexpected but perfect way?

Next ask: What did I do that worked?

Examples of responses (yours might be similar or quite different) are:

I took action on my own behalf quickly.

I stayed true to my vision, my belief in the potential for collaboration between the Universe and me.

I stayed in my heart.

I stayed grounded.

I reframed my fear so I could see the gift in the situation.

I stayed in my power.

I gave myself permission to have power.

I felt the gift.

I felt the support of the Universe.

I wasn't a victim.

Use EFT to change this Setup phrase:

Even though I have this repeating program in my life, because of those events that happened and the people who caused them, and it is making me mad and sad a lot...

to this:

I now know there is goodness in me, and there has always been goodness in me, and so I am making these other, better choices in my life now, and I am curious about how that starts happening, sometimes in surprising and unpredictable ways...

Add your positive statements:

And now I choose to take action quickly on my own behalf.

And now I choose to reframe my fear so that I can see the gift in the situation.

When you find yourself wanting to stand up for yourself in stronger, more effective ways, but you can feel confusion inside, try this approach. Begin by thinking of specific incidents in which you felt a conflict around taking some step or action. A part of you wants to do this, but another part of you is holding back. Or you feel a strong resistance to doing something that "everyone else" is doing or thinks you should do, and at the same time you want to please those people and you think you are a wimp for not just going for it. Make a list of times like this in your life, making sure you include incidents from your childhood.

Tap for each incident, for all the feelings you had, for all the beliefs about yourself that came up, for how your body felt then or feels now when you think of the incident, for any symptoms that seem related to the issue of standing up for yourself.

Use tapping phrases like:

Even though I'm not good at asking for what I need, or asking to be heard, I am choosing to honor myself and find alternative ways to accomplish what I want, while at the same time honoring what I need.

Even though it is not the right thing for me to _____, I honor my body's wisdom for making that clear to me.

Even though I don't think well on my feet, I can take a stand on my own behalf, and find different ways to achieve the same end.

Even though I really want their approval, I understand I'm not wimping out, in fact, I am taking a stand on my own behalf. This is a very brave act on the part of my feet (legs/back/knees). I am standing up for myself!

Even though I want their approval, I honor my need for connection, and connecting with myself is the most important act I can take.

Even though I feel all this fear, I choose to find other ways to honor my intentions that are more appropriate for me right now. Sometime in the future, I may choose to deal with the fear. It is up to me.

Include the 9 Gamut procedure in your tapping routines (see chapter 2 for how to do this). This procedure is a very good tool for helping the mind to reconsider and reprioritize the elements of an internal conflict. You don't need to say anything particular while you do the 9 Gamut tapping. Just start out with tapping on the back of the hand, and think for a moment about how to state the conflict. "On the one hand…but on the other hand…"

Practice noticing evidence of your own goodness this week!

Week Eight: Point Yourself in a Healing Direction— Celebrate Your Sensitivity!

We can stop obsessively tracking our failures. The engine that runs all this is our intention. We can turn ourselves in a healing direction. We can start paying attention to what we need in this very moment. We can be directed by our positive intention. We can change how we feel about being "too sensitive," and we can celebrate who we are. The world needs what we know!

Use this tapping script to turn yourself in a healing direction.

Even though I am used to tracking my failures, and the people I learned how to do this from were really good at it, I love and accept myself anyway.

Even though my family story is all about trying to prevent failures, I accept myself and I accept my family. We are all doing the best we can.

Even though I have to be perfect so that I don't fail, I accept myself, and I forgive myself for putting all this pressure on myself. I just haven't known any other way!

Even though failure is not allowed in my family, I accept myself and how I feel. I honor myself for how hard this has been for me.

Even though I can't speak up for myself…

Even though I fear that if I am noticed I will be judged…

Even though I worry what's wrong with me…

Especially because I deserve to, I am ready to dissolve this old approach to telling the story of my life. I intend to do this, starting in this moment!

Now repeat that tapping list that framed all the problems we experience from our sensitivity, and reframe them again as our gifts. Then we can make them even better!

Again, the following words are mine. Change them however you like to find phrases that fit you and feel good to you. Maybe you like to speak in superlatives—use those. Maybe you have more profound or more spiritual ways of expressing what is truly the best, loveliest, and greatest about you—go for it! Use your best words, ones that make you light up inside!

Tap using the normal EFT spots. But instead of saying "Even though…" try saying "Especially because…" Remove the old phrases in the parentheses and replace them in each case with what follows:

Especially because (I worry that I am too sensitive) I love that I am so sensitive, I choose to deepen and expand my sensitivity in powerful wonderful ways.

Especially because (I feel so deeply) I have this fabulous capacity to feel deeply, I choose to accept it as an honor and learn how to share what I know in ways that are helpful.

Especially because (I think my sensitivity is a weakness) I like that I am sensitive, I choose to love, appreciate, and honor this powerful, world-changing soul quality that I have been so blessed with. The world needs what I have to offer! I am ready to be more!

Especially because (I think something is wrong with me, that it is my fault) I believe that I am a good person, I choose to open to what I know in my deepest heart that I can become! I love, appreciate, and honor this precious being that I am!

Especially because (I wish things didn't bother me so much) I am glad that I am so aware, I choose to trust the Universe to handle the problems and I use my awareness and my energy to make a difference in this world that I care so much about.

Continue tapping beginning with the phrase "Especially because" (EB):

EB I have this wonderful gift of being able to think and speak in abstract big picture, profound concepts, I choose to deepen and strengthen my ability to be an "imagineer," and I use my manifestation ability even better so that the goodness I sense has a space to live in, in this world.

EB being cooperative and diplomatic is important to me, I choose to break the rules that aren't working for me and make new ones that feel right, in ways that still honor other people's integrity and intentions.

EB I hunger for deep and meaningful relationships, I make creating and maintaining a good and satisfying relationship with myself my first priority.

EB I value personal growth, authenticity, and integrity, I choose to discover my own strengths and excellence, and do everything I can to enlarge them.

EB I am internally deeply caring, I choose to take just as good care of myself as I do of _____.

EB I am deeply committed to the positive and the good, I choose to honor that commitment to myself!

EB I have a mission to bring peace to the world, I choose a mission of bringing peace into my own life.

EB I have a strong personal morality, I choose to stand even taller in my own strong life!

EB I often make extraordinary sacrifices for someone/something I believe in, I choose myself!

EB I think I am unusual and unique, I choose to stand up for myself and express who I am with love and a light heart. No one can resist that.

EB I have a good imagination, I choose to find amazing ways of bringing magic into my life where there was only misery before. Evolution itself depends on how good I get at this. The world needs what I have to offer!

Use this Eight-Week Program in the way that fits best for you. Take as long as you like on each "week." Make your own creative additions. Repeat the program after you finish it. Make it your own. Celebrate your sensitivity!

Appendix A:
What Doctors Say about the
Sensitive Temperament

I offer this book as an introduction to the concept of the highly sensitive temperament. I want to assist you, the reader, to ease your experience of sensitivity in a rather ignorant and sometimes hostile culture with EFT. And I want to invite you to consider the profound gifts that this trait offers to the world.

Most physicians and a high percentage of professionals in the helping fields are currently unaware of sensitivity as an actual emotional temperament. There does exist a small but growing body of scientific research on the trait of sensitivity, although, as you might expect, there are some disagreements among the academicians and researchers.

A physician whose radical ideas are gaining acceptance is Dr. John Sarno, professor of clinical rehabilitation medicine at the New York University School of Medicine, attending physician at the Howard A. Rusk Institute of Rehabilitation Medicine at the New York

University Medical Center, and author of numerous books on the mind-body connection, including *Healing Back Pain*.

John E. Sarno, MD: Emotions Are Held in the Body

Although Dr. Sarno doesn't speak about the sensitive temperament specifically, what he says about emotions held in the body is consistent with our approach to emotional issues with EFT.

Dr. Sarno's most notable (and controversial) achievement is the development, diagnosis, and treatment of tension myositis syndrome (TMS), which is not recognized by mainstream medical science. According to Dr. Sarno, TMS is a psychosomatic illness causing chronic back, neck, and limb pain that is not relieved by standard medical treatments. He cites other ailments, such as gastrointestinal problems, dermatological disorders, and repetitive-strain injuries, as TMS related.

Dr. Sarno reports that he has successfully treated more than ten thousand patients at the Rusk Institute by educating them on his beliefs of a psychological and emotional basis to their pain and symptoms. His theory is, in part, that the symptoms are an unconscious "distraction" from the deep emotional issues. He believes that when patients recognize that it is only a distraction, the symptoms then serve no purpose and go away.

Nancy Selfridge, MD, author of *Freedom from Fibromyalgia* and chief of the Complementary Medicine and Wellness Clinic in the Group Health HMO in

Madison, Wisconsin, spoke on the subject of the highly sensitive temperament and chronic pain at the 2005 conference of the Association for Comprehensive Energy Psychology (ACEP). Here is a partial transcript of her talk.

Healing the Sensitive Soul—
Live From Your Heart's Desire

By Nancy Selfridge, MD

I believe that chronic pain patients start out with a sensitive system to begin with, by birthright, temperamentally. One of the tests that I have administered in my practice is the Highly Sensitive Person test developed by Elaine Aron. All my patients scored high on this. And the other thing that I noted, if I asked my patients if they'd done a Myers-Briggs temperament inventory, they were, except for two patients in my recollection, Intuitive Feelers. The I or E and the P or J doesn't matter so much, but that NF function seems to identify a nervous system that has fewer filters on it than is considered the norm. [See chapter 1 in this book for an explanation of Myers-Briggs and what the letters denote.]

One of the things both Rue and I both try to do in our work is help people understand that it is OK to honor the sensitive temperament in order to be well. The literature says that people who are wired this way need periods of no and low stimulation in order to achieve homeostasis.

What is the difference between people who are highly sensitive and become chronically ill, and people who are highly sensitive and don't? I don't know. That's fascinating. I notice that my friends who are highly sensitive who have not gotten sick have made dramatically different lifestyle choices than I did. Some people have somehow gotten enough recognition, perhaps early in life, that it fortified them against the slings and arrows of normal fortune, much less outrageous fortune.

So how do the interventions work, when they do, if we use energy therapy? I believe when we change our thought patterns, we're going to see change in electrochemical flow in the brain from the limbic system. We can use some cognitive approaches, but we also can manipulate subtle energies. I think energy psychology techniques help to uncouple old established patterns that are translated into pain in our patients, and into autonomic dysfunction.

Patients ask me, how does this work? I tell them it is like running the defrag program on your computer. Something happened to you that triggered this real problem in your brain and overactivated this area in your brain. Now this area is sort of chaotic and fragmented with the information in there. When we do EFT, it is like running a good defrag. Maybe that model is not an accurate one, but it suffices.

If you take enough histories on chronic pain patients, you will inevitably find triggers, just as you do with posttraumatic stress disorder. We are looking at both stress and trauma here. If I ask, "When your symptoms started, what was going on in your life that might represent stress or trauma?" I may hear, "Oh, nothing."

I had one woman who came to see me for a chronic illness for at least two years on a regular basis. I explained the whole mind-body model of chronic pain, stress, and trauma to her. She kept saying there wasn't anything particularly difficult going on at the time that she became ill. One day she brought her husband, and I don't know why, but I asked her again. She still said that no, nothing was going on, and this guy's jaw dropped down to the floor.

I looked at him and said, "OK, what is it?" He looked at her and said "Nothing was happening? You were pregnant with twins, your mother was dying of cancer, you were her sole caretaker, she died, you gave birth to the twins, and one of them died." She said, "Well, I think I'm better from that."

So I found that you have to look at a patient's belief system.

We live in such a stressful culture, too. Remember the effects of this cultural container in which people are being held. I think the World Health Organization said that the number one epidemic in the world right now is stress. People are so stressed that they don't even recognize that they are feeling stress.

Since I have a sensitive temperament myself, medical school training was extremely stressful for me, but it didn't appear to make anybody else in my class sick. (Although, of course, some of them, now in their fifties, have coronary artery disease.) Kindergarten was okay for me, but first grade was horrible. I threw up at least three times a week for half a year, and still I kept going to school. School can be quite traumatic for a sensitive child.

We have these triggers and they can be single-event or cumulative stressors. I don't think it was a single traumatic event for me in training that created the triggers for me to become ill; I think it was just a lot piled on.

The neuroplasticity model for pain generation says that you can take an organism, let's say mammals, and you can subject that animal to a painful stimulus again and again, and the animal will begin responding with the pain response at lower and lower levels. So you start with a shock at ten and sooner or later you get down to a level of one, but the organism is still startling and responding with the pain response. I think this is sort of what we're seeing in chronic pain, although it may not take too many shocks.

Highly sensitive people are rare people. This is a nervous system that seems to have an element of vulnerability to stress and trauma anyway, maybe in the ways that the nervous system tends to be overactivated in our particular cultural context.

I have patients create an anger list, because the highly sensitive temperament, which is invested in benevolence, has a hard time acknowledging anger. Very often my patients will say, "I don't have any anger." I understand that, because I was very disconnected, too. When I did an anger journal for myself, I had to start with irritations and aggravations, and move on to rage.

We start with anger listing, and we do some journaling. Journaling about an emotional story has been shown to alleviate physical and psychological symptoms. Often three to seven journaling episodes are enough to create a shift.

It has become apparent to me that highly sensitive people are like canaries in the coal mine, responding to our stressful culture and environment with real illness and debilitation. There is nothing about this that is factitious, nor is it evidence of psychological disease or bad character. Chronic illness demands an expansion of our understanding of stress and disease.

As my own awareness of the multiple stressors we are exposed to increases, I expand my counseling of my sensitive patients to include diet and nutrition to avoid inflammation and illness, supplements to correct nutritional deficiencies, and diligent counseling about stress management strategies and interventions.

Most of all, I give permission to patients to live for their own hearts' desires, to explore their limiting beliefs, and to honor their sensitive temperaments. It is this latter path that will best help the sensitive soul from becoming sick again.

Speaking in depth about the highly sensitive child is not within the scope of this book. Here are some resources for you to explore the subject on your own.

Gary Craig, the founder of EFT, offers a lot of information on his website about using EFT with children (go to emofree.com and search on "children"). Here is a case story from the site to show you how EFT can help get children's feet firmly planted on a path of confidence.

A Four-Year-Old Heals Her Own Cough with EFT

Dear Gary,

I had the most amazing experience tonight driving home with my four-year-old daughter, Sydelle. We had been visiting my father, an EFT wiz and remarkable healer and before we left, she asked to do some EFT with him for her cough and sniffle. He helped guide her and proceeded with the usual process for children. It was gorgeous to observe her eagerly participating, repeating phrases Dad was saying most intently and cheerfully. There was a noticeable shift and her sniffle seemed less prominent.

We settled in the car for our drive home and this is when the real magic happened. Sydelle did EFT on her own all the way home (fifteen-minute drive), tapping and passionately using phrases Dad had used earlier, some of her own, and some she has heard Dad use with me and other clients. Some of the Setup statements and reminder phrases that Sydelle decided to use:

Even though I have this sniffle, Mummy and Daddy love me.

Even though I have this sniffle, my nana and nonno love me.

Even though I have this sniffle, I deeply and complete." (Her version of "I deeply and completely accept myself"—very cute! Also filled with intention, however.)

I no longer need this cough to be in my company.

Cough, go and live somewhere else.

Go away, cough, I don't want you anymore.

In between the Setups, she would do all her points, saying "this cough" or "this sniffle," and after three to four rounds she would test the intensity of her ailments by sniffing and coughing. The change was so dramatic! Her cough and sniff just kept improving and went from being chronic to barely even there. She just kept improving more and more each time she would test. By the time we got home, she was so much better it was unbelievable! Every night she had been coughing so badly, needing me to stay with her for a while and ohm to her. This night, not one cough or sniffle, just straight to sleep! Before she started tapping with Dad, her cough was a deep bark and I was having constantly to wipe her nose. Throughout her bedtime ritual, not a single cough or sniffle.

Even though I have always had the deepest faith in EFT and my father's capacity as a healer, never would I have dreamed that such a dramatic shift was possible in such a short amount of time. I feel so excited. Sydelle has been quite resistant to EFT, so we have not pushed her—I have surrogated for her in the past. Now she is ready and raring to go! She said to me, "Now I will have a good sleep, do a little more EFT in the morning, and then I will be completely better! I am going to do EFT every day from now on, Mamma." From the mouth of babes—no limitations, the sky is the limit.

Chantelle Boscarello, BA (Hons), LLB

For teaching EFT to children, see the article by Christine Metawati, "Teaching EFT to Children: A Detailed Account," under Resources on her website (metta center.com).

Elaine Aron, PhD, author of *The Highly Sensitive Child* and other books, offers good information about HST children as well as adults on her website (hsperson.com).

For a good article on parenting sensitive children, see "Parenting a Highly Sensitive Child," by Terri Goodwell, available on mothering.com.

Appendix C:
How Can a Practitioner Help
a Highly Sensitive Client?

If you are a practitioner, here are some ways to gather information for tapping with sensitive clients. They might want to learn more about their trait, and perhaps even tap for the feelings that being "so sensitive" have brought up in them. Help them to keep in mind that everything for them will be more vivid, more intense, and a deeper experience of pain or a richer experience of joy than it generally is for people who do not have a highly sensitive temperament.

If you are reading this as a highly sensitive person yourself, just imagine that you are your own practitioner, and follow along playing both parts. At the very least, this will give you lots of insights to explore further. If you work with a practitioner, you both can utilize what you have gathered here in your EFT sessions together.

One place to begin is by defining what it means to be highly sensitive.

Tap on the Definitions

Ask your client to take the Self-Test for the Highly Sensitive Person, developed by Elaine Aron, and reprinted in chapter 1, or mention some of the following descriptions of the temperament and ask, "Does this describe you?"

- You feel emotions deeply, and you can't hide what you feel.

- You are always aware of what people around you are feeling.

- Your feelings are easily hurt by criticism or even a look, and you keep thinking about what happened, what you might have done wrong, and what you should have done instead.

- You feel deeply for other people's suffering. It is difficult to watch the news, or to see sad movies.

- Sometimes you can slip easily into feeling anxious or depressed, and once caught in the feeling it is hard for you to move out of it.

- You are not comfortable in large crowds, hectic environments, or around loud music. You get easily overwhelmed when there is a lot going on.

- You are a perfectionist, and you want to be helpful —so much so that you put other people's needs ahead of your own.

- You do your best to avoid conflicts.

- You might feel like an alien in your own family. They are practical, industrious, and social, whereas you are quiet, imaginative, thoughtful ,and creative.

- You have a mission to bring peace to the world. You want to save the world from itself. You can see how good things could be, if only…

Make "positive" and "negative" lists about sensitivity, and tap on the lists.

When I have asked groups of sensitive people what they like best and least about their sensitive trait, I have gotten answers that reflect the qualities in the previous list. Some examples:

Drawbacks to being so sensitive:

- I notice more details, and when I comment on them people think I am weird.

- I am too attuned to what feels like impending criticism or disapproval.

- I feel socially awkward because I am not good at small talk.

- I am too empathic—I feel what everyone else is feeling.

- Being so sensitive makes me fearful.

- I seem to vibrate with the energy around me.

- I don't have good boundaries—I seem to become the other person.

- I lose myself.

- Every nuance of a situation penetrates me.

- I get nervous easily.

- I try to protect everyone.

- I worry about being a victim.

- I put other people's needs before mine.

  Blessings of being sensitive:

- I am intuitively aware of what another person may be thinking or feeling.

- Being sensitive is a great early warning system.

- Being so empathic makes me very understanding.

- I can "step into another's shoes."

- I am able to see/sense to the heart of a matter.

- I am deeply attuned to beauty.

- The "poetry" of everything comes through.

- I have a deep connection with spirit.

- I have a richer set of experiences than some others might.

- I have a different, more finely tuned sense of humor that is deeper and more readily available.

- I can see the beauty in almost anything.

- I see wholeness, always, everywhere.

You might begin later rounds of tapping with "Especially because…" and follow that with some of the positive phrases in the client's list.

Ask Evocative Questions and Tap on the Responses

I have found it helpful while working with someone to hold a kind of map in my mind of the experience of being highly sensitive. It helps me to ask the right questions so I know what we might focus on. These questions, described in chapters 7 and 8, are the elements of the map:

Question: What broke your heart?

Painful experiences are felt more deeply by a sensitive person, especially as a child.

Question: What did this experience lead you to believe about yourself, or what it is like to be in the world?

Experiences lead to beliefs. Those heartbreaking experiences, large and small, can lead to beliefs about who we are and what is possible for us in life.

Question: What emotions and feelings does this experience bring up in you?

It may not be possible or safe to express the powerful anger, sadness, fear, and shame that we feel during and after these painful experiences. Those feelings get stuffed or swallowed. Stuffed feelings show up later in our lives as physical and emotional pain and illness. Most people with chronic physical and emotional pain are highly sensitive. The fear of confronting powerful feelings can stop us from beginning a healing journey.

Question: What did your family believe about you being "so sensitive"? Were they trying to toughen you up for a tough world? Did your sensitivity threaten their own carefully covered up or denied sensitivity?

The people in our families who mistreated us did so because that is how they were treated, and these were the beliefs and feelings they themselves took on from their own family experience. The tendency to replicate these misunderstandings and illnesses gets passed down through the generations of a family. Our families had beliefs and feelings about being so sensitive, toughing it out, not standing out, or "making you strong."

Question: How can you take care of yourself and your needs without thinking that you are selfish? How could taking care of yourself first be a good thing? (Hint: I like to think of selfish as spelled "Self-ish," meaning "care of the Soul" or "self-care.")

Healing our family's history is on the way to healing the world! We just thought we had to start with healing the whole world so that it would be a safe place for us. That was pretty exhausting. We left ourselves off our own to-do list! Our personal healing can heal the whole family history.

Use Open-ended Sentences

As you know by now, being made to feel wrong unless you are taking care of everyone else first is a typical experience of the highly sensitive person. And so, even when we are hurting, we tough it out and soldier on.

I had to sacrifice myself for _____ or else _____.

I had to tough it out and soldier on _____ or else _____.

Reframe Sensitivity and Tap on Your Insights

When a sensitive person chooses a life event to explore with EFT, here is another way to tap to reframe the sensitive response to what happened in an incident. Of course, these questions will be evocative no matter what the issue or how sensitive the individual. The underlying supposition to begin with is:

Even though I don't see how I could reframe this event positively, I am open to seeing it differently, and I'm open to seeing purpose and wisdom in the event and in my own and others' responses, and I deeply and completely love and accept myself, no matter what.

1. How did you respond to the event itself? (tap)

   What were your emotions, thoughts, and/or body's response? (tap)

2. How did other people respond to the event? (tap)

   How do you feel/think about your (and others') response? (tap)

3. What regrets, sorrow, or other feelings do you have about the event and its effect on you and your life? (e.g., If only I had known, I wouldn't have suffered/wasted my life/limited myself.) (tap)

4. Would things have gone differently if you (and others) had known you are highly sensitive? (tap)

   Now that you understand that you are highly sensitive, what would you (and others) do differently in response to the event? (tap)

5. From the perspective of a wise, sensitive advisor to yourself, what wisdom do you see in your (and others') response? (tap)

6. What does the event and your response mean about you and your capacity to respond to life now? (tap)

What was the positive intention of your (and others') response at the time? What were you trying to get for yourself? (tap)

Ellen: How One Person Answered These Questions and Tapped for Her Responses

Here are some of the answers that one client, now in her fifties, gave to the questions as she considered the effect on her life of having been raped in her senior year of high school. An EFT tapping Setup phrase can be created out of each of these answers.

How did you respond to the event? What were your emotions and thoughts?

Trauma, shock, alone, afraid, confused, felt stupid, tricked.

The dreams of my life were shattered.

I identified with the upset feelings of my parents more than my own feelings.

All I wanted to do was protect my father, his reputation.

Others' responses:

No one knew how to deal with it.

My mother was in shock and couldn't respond.

My father wanted to deal with the situation but keep it quiet because of the effect it would have on his career.

My parents did the best they could.

If I had known I was sensitive:

I come from a family of warriors that has had to hide their identity.

Pay attention to the real me, not the story about me.

I could say, "Stop—I am the one who was hurt here."

I am not as invincible as I seem.

My mother would have been able to be there for me.

I could ask to be held.

I thought I had to—and could—protect everyone.

I didn't know that I didn't know how to be safe.

I would not have been tricked into the situation to begin with.

I would have found help in healing the trauma at the time, rather than allowing it to shape my whole subsequent life.

Wise advisor perspective:

You were so aware of your father's stresses, and you so wanted to help.

You were not meant to be here to sacrifice for others.

Treat yourself as worthy.

You are worth being protected.

You can still care for others.

You can live from that knowing of your own worth.

Be empathic, continue to feel deeply, but your first priority is to protect yourself.

This experience taught me to stand up for myself:

I realize that when I speak up for others, I am really wanting to speak up for myself.

I know how to walk away now.

That experience blasted me out of the shell that had been holding me in place.

The blessing is in understanding my sensitivity trait instead of going to blame, shame, or "I have wasted my life."

EFT is the perfect tool for you, as a sensitive person, to learn how to "deeply and completely love and accept" yourself. You are not introverted; you are reserved, self-contained, and independent. You are not shy; you love and intend to create deep and meaningful interaction. It is remarkable that when we change our perception of ourselves, we automatically change our perception of the world. And then the world changes!

Even though I don't see how I could reframe this event positively, I'm open to seeing it differently, and I'm open to seeing purpose and wisdom in the event and in my own and others' responses, and I deeply and completely love and accept myself, no matter what.

A Practitioner Shares her Experience: "It's an Honor to Work with Sensitive People"

by Margaret M. Lynch

Margaret Lynch, an EFT practitioner and coach who was learning about the concept of the sensitive temperament wrote me some wonderful e-mails about her experience of working with sensitive clients. She has some very good ideas that other practitioners might want to take note of, so here are her e-mails compiled in an essay:

Once I realize I am working with a sensitive temperament, I can adapt my approach and everything I say. This framework of understanding allows such a greater level of rapport and healing, even in the first appointment. They feel validated and understood in a way they often have not experienced before. This alone is quite triggering for them! Now I have a unique respect for sensitive people, their journey and the people in my personal life whom I now see differently.

In a first appointment with a client, there is usually some giveaway or hint that I may be dealing with a sensitive temperament. I then change my line of questioning along the lines of the checklist you provide in your work, to confirm if they are a sensitive temperament and how highly they score.

Sometimes they hide it well and it comes out later in session. As I explain the idea that there is a sensitive temperament type and they score highly, that there are lots of people like them, and what the attributes are, I am careful to watch their intensity because this information itself can be a shock. It can be overwhelming to suddenly feel understood, validated, and not alone. I honor that. Although it seems like it should be wonderful and validating, it can be overwhelming for the client. My goal is to build rapport and let them know that I understand, and use this understanding as a framework for working with them. If it seems overly triggering, I will hold off and bring out more in subsequent sessions.

Throughout the sessions, I find it is always triggering to say words about honoring their sensitivity or honoring that certain events were particularly difficult for them because of their temperament. Again, it's as if feeling finally understood causes great emotion in itself. I am careful to use these words, which come mostly from your "especially because" reframes, when I feel they are ready to hear them. I have learned to be more carefully in tune with their shifts to use these beautiful, empowering words only when they will allow the transformative impact that I have seen clients have.

I always refer these clients to your website and give them your "Especially because" reframes (crediting you), but I sometimes wait till the second or third session to give it to them.

But when they are ready, watch out, because the HST is naturally very advanced at spiritual work. Saying these beautiful words of yours really impacts them. Some of my HST clients have been more inspiring to me than I could imagine being to them!

One lesson I learned the hard way with highly sensitive people is to be more careful at the end of the session. Usually, this is the point with clients that I really lay on the positive reframes, honoring the self, becoming more oneself, especially in recognition that the clients are in a light hypnotic trance and are highly suggestible. I have, however, inadvertently triggered clients with what I think is going to be uplifting and beautiful. It seems as though they have not been "themselves" for so long, it is too much of a beautiful leap. My goal at the end is to finish things off, not stir things up. So I adjust my words to actually be a bit more flat.

I now have my first sensitive temperament client that has manifested fibromyalgia and I would like to share some details of the first two appointments. She was in so much overwhelm from past traumas and current deaths in her family that the first session was high emotional release. Despite my best efforts to minimize pain, she was still raw at the end. This is not a preferred scenario at the end of a session. We scheduled the next appointment for early the next week due to the amount of overwhelm and that she was still raw.

At her second appointment, she had taken my suggestion and gone through your website. Just reading your website and feeling validated and understood, by a credible source, was transformative and relieving for her. A real revelation, and she enjoyed reading it to her husband, too! She looked at your books and felt she was not ready to read them yet—too triggering. But I have to thank you on her behalf, because your words really impacted her and I was able to leverage that during the session. I also recommended she do one of your teleseminars and have that experience as well.

The approach I took for the second session was to reduce the raw feeling and focus on some specific, more annoying events, instead of going right back to the biggies. Also to bring in more calm and peace to alleviate the raw feeling. She admitted feeling resistant to going through what she thought would be more pain. She wanted more peace, more calm, and I thought this was more important than marching on to more trauma (soldiering on).

I wanted to tell you about two techniques I tried that seemed to work well.

One of the annoying situations in her life was around a couple of other people treating her badly, being obnoxious, but she had to deal with them to get something done. So after reducing that intensity, I thought about adding in protection for her, since this type of confrontational person is difficult for the sensitive temperament.

We tapped around phrases starting with "seeing him as coming from a place of unmet needs" and then going to "him, way over there, throwing a tantrum, like a child, over there, apart from me, for his reasons, and I am over here, way over here, separate, in my space, in my peace, caring less, feeling safe and calm in my own separate bubble of calm and peace, in my own light, in my energy, and he's over there louder before but quieter now, dimmer, quieter, less important to me and who I am."

This allowed her to start visualizing that distance, and she could imagine a protective bubble around her. This gave me an idea! I said, "Rue believes that sensitive people are special, doesn't she? She believes that they have a light and a mission because of their sensitive temperament." She agreed.

I continued, "You are a creative, compassionate, imaginative person who feels things deeply. That means you are so close to source, aren't you? Because that connection to your source is your stream of imagination, inspiration, and creativity, which some people go their whole lives not ever feeling."

Wheels were turning, she was listening, processing, agreeing. I continued, "Your connection to source is so strong by your very nature. Let's tap into your connection to source, light, energy, God, to bring you even more of that light so it can surround you and keep you in your peace."

She loved it, so we tapped on visualizing that the light from the center of her, all around her, above her, that draws through her very nature as a sensitive person, could be called upon to grow stronger and surround her in a cocoon of light, safety, peace, and harmony. Calm and peaceful within the safety, within that personal light, she was safe to start becoming more her.

We also mixed in tapping on "honoring the value of me, I was put here for a purpose, part of me knows this as a deeper truth, part of me is still resisting it, that's OK." I had to watch closely as this can become triggering for a sensitive person, so it was just a touch.

She said this was like a light bulb going off for her and she had never thought of her sensitivity and creativity as a conduit or connection to source for the very peace she sought. She even had a vision of her mother (passed) who was joining in and sending her more light.

It is such an honor to work with sensitive people and their exceptional hearts and desire for healing!

Margaret Lynch's website is newenglandsuccess coaching.com.

Healing the Healer: Addicted to Love

I think of my work with someone as a co-creative partnership. I do it because it deeply satisfies my love of a kind of snowboarding for the spirit: a hanging-out-on-the-edge-of-the-unknown-always-open-to-revelation state of being. This work creates a deep grounding in my body as a portal for connection: to my own deep self, to another being, to the spirit of the earth, to the chalice of what is possible.

I used to be a Fixer. Especially when I began to fill a toolbox with all these useful tools that helped people make real lasting changes in their lives. It actually began to seem possible not only to save the world, but also to save souls. What radiant, seductive power!

I would venture to say that most practitioners in the helping professions are of the sensitive temperament. Highly sensitive people always have a deep inner sense of mission to bring healing to the world. We want to fix what is wrong—now! We can see what is wrong. And we know how to fix it! But that strong urge is something of which we need to become aware, because it so easily goes out of balance.

When someone tells me about a problem he or she is having, I can feel a response rising in me that wants to make things right. I might find myself falling into an archetypal self-image: the Healer, or the Compassionate One, or the Rescuing Knight. (Alternatively, the complexity of the problem might throw me into the Disempowered One, or the Failure, the "This-is-Beyond- Me" persona, or maybe the Hider or the Retreater.)

I know that when I respond as the Fixer, it is an automatic response to the energy of the problem. I become caught in an unconscious response that isn't healthy for me or anyone else. Ultimately, being a Fixer drains me and blocks my access to the creative, out-of-the-box kind of thinking in which the opening, untying energy lives.

I had to learn how to free myself from my inner Fixer, the part of me that wanted to Save the World. (You know the drill: The whole world has to be saved and made safe to live in before I can tend to my own needs.) Working with this I could feel thick brown cords that had grown from my heart to bind me to clients in a way that saw them as broken and me as able to be expert, authority, savior. I felt these cords dissolve and be replaced by radiant streams of light that flowed through me to the person I was working with, nourishing me with joy and a bright sense of creative fun. This was a powerful inner experience for me.

In the years since then, I have come to understand this experience more deeply. What I felt in that healing moment was the seed for a sense of connecting love that respects and enhances both me and the person sitting there with me. I have come to understand that my first order of business as a healer is to maintain my integrity, wholeness, and sovereignty.

I have the capacity to assist in another's healing. But there must be nothing in me that gets in the way of honoring the client's right to be who he or she is: a sacred and sovereign human being that I share the earth with, in this time or another. I can't need to heal anyone. "Fixing" others isn't good for them, or me.

Being a mother has probably taught me more about working in this way than anything else I have ever done.

Mothering for me has been about finding the fine balance of letting someone know that you love them wholeheartedly, unabashedly, even while you disagree with them, at the same time that you allow them to do what they feel is right for them, while still expressing your own opinion about it, but not in a way that restricts them from learning how to act from their own will, and absolutely not just to please you. Holding them in your heart while freeing them to be fully them. (Marriage/partnership is a pretty good classroom for this, too.)

The issue here is about where in us our response is drawn from. In any situation—in my work, in my family, in the world—I can draw energy from the part of me that looks for problems and sees them everywhere, and goes into complain, attack, or fix-it mode. Or I can activate the part of me that looks for how a thing is working itself through and changing, seeking what goodness is trying to emerge—untwisting, untying, and smoothing—and set myself to assist in that process, rather invisibly.

In *The Four-Fold Way*, cultural anthropologist Angeles Arrien, PhD, says this about the Healer: "The archetype of the Healer is a universal mythic structure that all human beings experience. Among indigenous cultures the Healer supports the principle of paying attention to what has heart and meaning. Healers in all major traditions recognize that the power of love is the most potent healing force available to all human beings. Effective Healers from any culture are those who extend the arms of love: acknowledgment, acceptance, recognition, validation, gratitude."

Dr. Arrien views addiction as the shadow aspect of the Healer. At its deepest positive intention, addictive behavior would seem to be about seeking spirit, a sense of connection, feeling like you belong, anything that generates a sense of purpose, power, and peace.

Whatever it is that brings us these feelings can be seductive, whether it is alcohol or drugs, and even—or maybe especially and initially— admiration, being needed, being looked up to as a savior, a healer, a fixer. The sensitive temperament often has addictive tendencies.

Dr. Arrien's research suggests that human beings share four basic addictive patterns, each of which masks a positive intention that she calls the "unclaimed human resource":

- **The addiction to intensity.** The unclaimed human resource is the expression of love.

- **The addiction to perfection.** The unclaimed human resource is the expression of excellence and right use of power.

- **The addiction to the need to know.** The unclaimed human resource is the expression of wisdom.

- **The addiction to being fixated on what is not working rather than what is working.** The unclaimed human resource is the expression of vision and ways of looking at the whole.

Often the people who walk through my door or call me for help on the telephone are people in the helping, fixing, serving professions themselves. Often they themselves suffer from addictions to behaviors or substances. I think of them as being addicted to love. Looking for love in all the wrong places, as it were.

I worked with a highly sensitive man recently who typifies this. He is an AODA (Alcohol and Other Drug Abuse) counselor who continues to battle his own addiction to painkillers, among other deep-rooted issues in his life. He was seeing various professionals for those problems. He came to me because his soul was in pain and I offer something different from what his doctors and psychotherapist offer.

In a recent session, we had a conversation about how hard it is for him to set boundaries with his clients. He gets easily and too deeply drawn into their lives. "When someone is willing to 'go to bat' with me, work with me, I become willing to do anything for them," he said. "I put my own priorities aside. But then that opens a door that I can't shut. I begin to feel attacked, and it makes a kind of poison in me. I begin to experience a chemical reaction in my body and then I get very sick, emotionally and physically. I don't know how to tell which clients are going to be toxic for me."

I asked him to think of two clients that he worked with as a counselor, one who was the kind of person that became toxic for him and one with whom he knew not to get too involved.

He described Ellen and Steve, respectively. Ellen was initially resistant, so he had to really work to connect with her. "She really needs help, she really needs my help. I start to think, what can I do for her? I am one of the very few who can do what needs to be done. I am there 100 percent for her. When there is a breakthrough in her resistance, any step forward, it blows my self-esteem way up when she responds to me. It makes me feel high—warm, fuzzy, hyper. I feel like I am shot up with something. My body gets energy. It's like being on coke, or heroin. That feeling tricks me. I get way into helping her before I realize that I am overwhelmed, and then the toxic reactions in me start and I am totally a victim to them."

His description of Steve started out the same way, but quickly diverged. He said, "I start with the willingness to be there for him. In the same way as Ellen, he needs my help, and as I become more useful to him I get a feeling of being powerful, an excited, warm fuzzy feeling, radiant. But then there is a 'zap.'"

I asked him to be aware of how the zap shows up in his body. He thought about it, and then said he first could hear the zap in Steve's voice, by "his tone and then his narcissistic, negative, guilt-tripping, manipulative talk. I can feel the warm fuzzy feeling getting tainted. I start to squirm when I talk to him. There is an all-over, internal murky feeling. I find myself stepping back."

Just becoming conscious of how he was seduced by his need to feel useful, powerful, worthy, and loved was important to this man. He has physiological cues now that will help him recognize his own body's warning signs way before he gets drawn in so far that he gets a toxic reaction. He can utilize his sensitivity to lead him away from being a Fixer, and toward just being centered in himself. The presence he radiates when he is just present in himself helps his clients find that quality in themselves, naturally.

These are themes that any of us who are drawn to doing healing work will encounter in many ways over time. Feeling needed is such a powerful draw. And for a sensitive temperament, the deep work with another person can be like food for the soul that is starving for connection. It is so important to become aware of our own beliefs and behaviors, and to turn ourselves toward transforming anything that is out of balance. The more we are able to "deeply and completely love and accept" ourselves as a fluid, generative continual emergence of the best in us, the more effective we will be in being present for our clients.

Practitioners are often fearful of not knowing enough to do this work. I don't think that is the issue at all. I believe that as practitioners we are asked, above all, to be present in the moment, quiet in the mind, open in the heart, and full with the trust that healing wants to happen, always. And then the right words, the right questions, the right silence are all just there.

To return to Dr. Arrien's description of the Healer: "The archetype of the Healer is a universal mythic structure that all human beings experience. Among indigenous cultures the Healer supports the principle of paying attention to what has heart and meaning. Healers in all major traditions recognize that the power of love is the most potent healing force available to all human beings. Effective Healers from any culture are those who extend the arms of love: acknowledgment, acceptance, recognition, validation, gratitude."

Couldn't this be a good definition of EFT in the hands of a person with a highly sensitive temperament?

EFT Glossary

The following terms have specific meanings in EFT. They are referred to in some of the reports included here and are often mentioned in EFT reports.

Acupoints. Acupuncture points which are sensitive points along the body's meridians. Acupoints can be stimulated by acupuncture needles or, in acupressure, by massage or tapping. EFT is an acupressure tapping technique.

Art of Delivery. The sophisticated presentation of EFT that uses imagination, intuition, and humor to quickly discover and treat the underlying causes of pain and other problems. The art of delivery goes far beyond Mechanical EFT.

Aspects are "issues within issues," different facets or pieces of a problem that are related but separate. When new aspects appear, EFT can seem to stop working. In truth, the original EFT treatment continues to work while the new aspect triggers a new set of symptoms. In some cases, many aspects of a situation or problem each require their own EFT treatment. In others, only a few do.

Basic Formula. See Mechanical EFT.

Basic Recipe. A four-step treatment consisting of Setup phrase, Sequence (tapping on acupoints in order), 9-Gamut Treatment, and Sequence. This was the original EFT protocol.

Borrowing Benefits. When you tap with or on behalf of another person, your own situation improves, even though you aren't tapping for your own situation. This happens in one-on-one sessions, in groups, and when you perform surrogate or proxy tapping. The more you tap for others, the more your own life improves.

Chasing the Pain. After applying EFT, physical discomforts can move to other locations and/or change in intensity or quality. A headache described as a sharp pain behind the eyes at an intensity of 8 might shift to dull throb in back of the head at an intensity of 7 (or 9, or 3 or any other intensity level). Moving pain is an indication that EFT is working. Keep "chasing the pain" with EFT and it will usually go to zero or some low number. In the process, emotional issues behind the discomforts are often successfully treated.

Chi. *Chi,* or energy, flows through and around every living being. It is said to regulate spiritual, emotional, mental, and physical balance and to be influenced by *yin* (the receptive, feminine force) and *yang* (the active masculine force). These forces, which are complementary opposites, are in constant motion. When *yin* and *yang* are balanced, they work together with the natural flow of *chi* to help the body achieve and maintain health. *Chi* moves through the body along invisible pathways, or channels, called meridians. Traditional Chinese Medicine identifies 20 meridians along which chi or vital energy flows or circulates through to all parts of the body. Acupoints along the meridians can be stimulated to improve the flow of *Chi* and, in EFT, to resolve emotional issues.

Choices Method. Dr. Patricia Carrington's method for inserting positive statements and solutions into Setup and Reminder Phrases.

Core Issues. Core issues are deep, important underlying emotional imbalances, usually created in response to traumatic events. A core issue is truly the crux of the problem, its root or heart. Core issues are not always obvious but careful detective work can often uncover them, and once discovered, they can be broken down into specific events and handled routinely with EFT.

Generalization Effect. When related issues are neutralized with EFT, they often take with them issues that are related in the person's mind. In this way, several issues can be resolved even though only one is directly treated.

Global. While the term "global" usually refers to something that is universal or experienced worldwide, In EFT it refers to problems, especially in Setup phrases, that are vague and not specific.

Intensity Meter. The zero-to-10 scale that measures pain, discomfort, anger, frustration, and every other physical or emotional symptom. Intensity can also be indicated with gestures, such as hands held close together (small discomfort) or wide apart (large discomfort).

Mechanical EFT. EFT's Basic Formula consists of tapping on the Karate Chop point or Sore Spot while saying three times, "Even though I have this ___[problem]___ , I fully and complete accept myself" (Setup phrase), followed by tapping the Sequence of EFT acupoints in order, with an appropriate Reminder Phrase.

Meridians. Invisible channels or pathways through which energy or *Chi* flows in the body. The eight primary meridians pass through five pairs of vital organs, and twelve secondary meridians network to the extremities. The basic premise of EFT is that the cause of every negative emotion and most physical symptoms is a block or disruption in the flow of *Chi,* or energy, along one or more of the meridians.

Movie Technique, or Watch a Movie Technique. In this process you review in your mind, as though it were a movie, a bothersome specific event. When intensity comes up, stop and tap on that intensity. When the intensity subsides, continue in your mind with the story. This method has been a mainstay in the tool box of many EFT practitioners. It may be the most-often used EFT technique of all. For a full description, see www.emofree.com/tutorial/tutorcthree.htm

Personal Peace Procedure. An exercise in which you clear problems and release core issues by writing down, as quickly as possible, as many bothersome events from your life that you can remember. Try for at least 50 or 100. Give each event a title, as though it is a book or movie. When the list is complete, begin tapping on the largest issues. Eliminating at least one uncomfortable memory per day (a very conservative schedule) removes at least 90 unhappy events in three months. If you work through two or three per day, it's 180 or 270. For details, see www.emofree.com/tutorial/tutormthirteen.htm.

Reminder Phrase. A word, phrase, or sentence that helps the mind focus on the problem being treated. It is used in combination with acupoint tapping.

Setup phrase, or Setup. An opening statement said at the beginning of each EFT treatment which defines and helps neutralize the problem. In EFT, the standard Setup phrase is, "Even though I have this _____, I fully and completely accept myself."

Story Technique, or Tell a Story Technique. Narrate or tell the story out loud of a specific event dealing with trauma, grief, anger, etc., and stop to tap whenever the story becomes emotionally intense. Each of the stopping points represents another aspect of the issue that, on occasion, will take you to even deeper issues. This technique is identical to the Movie Technique except that in the Movie Technique, you simply watch past events unfold in your mind. In the Tell a Story Technique, you describe them out loud.

Surrogate or Proxy Tapping involves tapping on yourself on behalf of another person. The person can be present or not. Another way to perform surrogate or proxy tapping is to substitute a photograph, picture, or line drawing for the person and tap on that.

Tail-enders. The "yes, but" statements that create negative self-talk. When you state a goal or affirmation, tail-enders point the way to core issues.

Tearless Trauma Technique. This is another way of approaching an emotional problem in a gentle way. It involves having the client guess as to the emotional intensity of a past event rather than painfully re-live it mentally.

Writings on Your Walls. Limiting beliefs and attitudes that result from cultural conditioning or family attitudes, these are often illogical and harmful yet very strong subconscious influences.

Yin and Yang. See *Chi,* above.

Index